UNDERSTANDING
LARRY McMURTRY

UNDERSTANDING CONTEMPORARY AMERICAN LITERATURE

Matthew J. Bruccoli, Founding Editor

Linda Wagner-Martin, Series Editor

UNDERSTANDING

LARRY McMURTRY

Steven Frye

The University of South Carolina Press

© 2017 University of South Carolina

Published by the University of South Carolina Press
Columbia, South Carolina 29208

www.sc.edu/uscpress

Manufactured in the United States of America

26 25 24 23 22 21 20 19 18 17
10 9 8 7 6 5 4 3 2 1

Library of Congress Cataloging-in-Publication Data

Names: Frye, Steven, author.
Title: Understanding Larry McMurtry / Steven Frye.
Description: Columbia : The University of South Carolina Press, 2017. |
  Series: Understanding contemporary American literature | Includes
  bibliographical references and index.
Identifiers: LCCN 2016054278 (print) | LCCN 2016054681 (ebook) |
  ISBN 9781611177626 (hardback) | ISBN 9781611177633 (ebook)
Subjects: LCSH: McMurtry, Larry—Criticism and interpretation. |
  BISAC: LITERARY CRITICISM / American / General. | PERFORMING ARTS /
  Film & Video / Screenwriting.
Classification: LCC PS3563.A319 Z66 2017 (print) | LCC PS3563.A319 (ebook) |
  DDC 813/.54—dc23
LC record available at https://lccn.loc.gov/2016054278

This book was printed on recycled paper with
30 percent postconsumer waste content.

For Kristin, Melissa, and Thomas,
with love

CONTENTS

SERIES EDITOR'S PREFACE

The Understanding Contemporary American Literature series was founded by the estimable Matthew J. Bruccoli (1931–2008), who envisioned these volumes as guides or companions for students as well as good nonacademic readers, a legacy that will continue as new volumes are developed to fill in gaps among the nearly one hundred series volumes published to date and to embrace a host of new writers only now making their marks on our literature.

As Professor Bruccoli explained in his preface to the volumes he edited, because much influential contemporary literature makes special demands, "the word understanding in the titles was chosen deliberately. Many willing readers lack an adequate understanding of how contemporary literature works; that is, of what the author is attempting to express and the means by which it is conveyed." Aimed at fostering this understanding of good literature and good writers, the criticism and analysis in the series provide instruction in how to read certain contemporary writers—explicating their material, language, structures, themes, and perspectives—and facilitate a more profitable experience of the works under discussion.

In the twenty-first century Professor Bruccoli's prescience gives us an avenue to publish expert critiques of significant contemporary American writing. The series continues to map the literary landscape and to provide both instruction and enjoyment. Future volumes will seek to introduce new voices alongside canonized favorites, to chronicle the changing literature of our times, and to remain, as Professor Bruccoli conceived, contemporary in the best sense of the word.

Linda Wagner-Martin, Series Editor

CHAPTER 1

Understanding Larry McMurtry

After years away from home—writing novels, running his own bookstore in Washington, D.C., consulting on film adaptations of his many works—Larry McMurtry returned to Archer City, a small town in north Texas that had sustained itself for more than a hundred years on the cotton trade, ranching, and the oil industry. Archer City is in many ways an emblem of the American small town: vibrant and hopeful at its inception, a gathering place for trade and extravagant hope, wistful in its twilight as the pace of urbanization took people elsewhere. Like many towns throughout the country, it remains alive and by no means warrants an epitaph. But a description of it might best emerge from the language of historical memory. In Willa Cather's terms, Archer City takes its deepest breath from "the precious, the incommunicable, past." McMurtry's departure and return should come as no surprise, because of course he never really left. Some of his most memorable novels transform Archer City into the fictional Thalia and Anarene, and, like many American authors before him, he found that to leave was the best way to stay. Distance seems to inspire that peculiar alchemy of imagination and understanding that in the end amounts to wisdom and beauty.

In many of his important works, Larry McMurtry portrays his native Texas, both past and present, with a vivid unvarnished realism and, in doing so, imbues the region with a meaning perhaps not immediately observable to the naked eye. Barren range becomes the interior landscape of mind, full of natural detail and texture, a strangely permanent resource of personal identity. For McMurtry, Texas always remains itself, but it emerges also as a grand symbol for the American West and indeed the nation as a whole.[1] McMurtry's capacity to create characters bound in time and place but richly interior in their psychological complexity places him alongside the most notable practitioners of the novel form. People remain his primary subject—living, breeding, working, bleeding, and dying, always seeking, deeply flawed but sympathetic, frequently comic and endearing. They are universals to be found anywhere, yet they are distinctly American in their intense capacity for hope, their commonality, and their humble grandeur. As an author grounded in the novel form, Larry Mc-Murtry has become that rarity among contemporary authors: a popular novelist to be compared with some of the finest architects of the human drama.

Life and Career

Larry Jeff McMurtry, the son of William Jefferson McMurtry Jr. and Hazel McIver McMurtry, was born in Wichita Falls, Texas, in 1936 and was raised in Archer County, Texas, where he was first exposed to the people and places he would later fictionalize in many of his novels. He was only one generation or so removed from the age of the great cattle drives, and much of the culture remained, transposed in certain ways into the time of the oil derrick but retaining many of its former cultural contours: the roughness, violence, intolerance, the emphasis on courage and hard work, even the religious fundamentalism. He was also exposed to a practice that influenced more than his themes and permeates his writerly practice—storytelling and humor laced with elements of the tall tale. These experiences, together with the historical circumstances of historical change in the Southwest that he observed, became central to his work. Located near Archer City, his first home was remote and rural. McMurtry's grandparents, who were originally from Missouri, moved into the area in 1889, buying a parcel of ranch land near Windthorst, eighteen miles from Archer City. His parents first made their home on the paternal ranch, and McMurtry lived there until he was six years old. His mother wanted a more social environment where she could indulge her love of bridge and conversation, and in 1942 she convinced McMurtry's father to move the family to Archer City, where McMurtry's three siblings were born. Archer City was a fairly typical small town of its time, tremendously religious, preoccupied with rigid moral codes with respect to sexuality, highly provincial and insular. Thus, in his childhood, McMurtry alternated from the open range to a provincial American town. In his earliest years, he felt vaguely out of place among the rough, independent, hardworking, yet anti-intellectual West Texans who lived in the outlying country. Always by his own admission "bookish," he experienced the writer's capacity to observe and remove, which served him well later and fostered his ability to draw the interiors and exteriors of his often idiosyncratic characters. McMurtry's childhood was not atypical, and he seems to have demonstrated a range of abilities and interests. In high school, he participated in sports, lettering three years in basketball and one year in baseball. He was a member of the 4-H Club for four years and was both the editor of and a writer for the school publication *Cat's Claw*. Many of his contemporaries in youth became the prototypes for his characters. One of his female classmates, Ceil Slack Cleveland, is thought by many scholars to be the basis for Jacy Farrow in *The Last Picture Show* (1966). Another classmate, Bobby Stubbs, was the pattern for Sonny Crawford in the same novel and for Duane Moore in *Texasville* (1981) and *Duane's Depressed* (1999) and, according to McMurtry, inspired other characters as well. McMurtry and Stubbs were apparently close, and before Stubbs's death, in the early 1990s, McMurtry inscribed books to him. In 1954 McMurtry graduated with honors from Archer City High School and enrolled for a short time at Rice University, in Houston, later transferring to North Texas State College (now the University of North Texas), where he studied literature and worked on student publications, including the unauthorized *Coexistence Review* and the student journal *Avesta*. At that time, he began writing short stories.

In 1959 McMurtry married Jo Ballard Scott, and the couple had one son, James Lawrence McMurtry (named after Henry James and D. H. Lawrence), before divorcing, in 1966. While married to Scott, McMurtry earned an M.A. degree from Rice University, having written his master's thesis, "Ben Jonson's Feud with the Poetasters: 1599–1601." He was awarded a prestigious Wallace Stegner creative writing fellowship at Stanford University, where he became friends with Chris Koch (the author of *The Year of Living Dangerously*) and Ken Kesey (the author of *One Flew over the Cuckoo's Nest*). McMurtry ultimately dedicated *In a Narrow Grave* to Kesey. He was a member of a group of writers who ultimately became widely recognized, including Tillie Olsen, Ernest Gaines, Robert Stone, and Wendell Berry. This experience seems to have contributed immensely to his development as a writer, giving him exposure to other emerging authors and the publishing community. In 1961 he returned to Texas and taught at Texas Christian University, in Fort Worth, as well as at Rice University, and he continued teaching intermittently throughout the 1960s while writing and publishing his earliest works. During his time at Rice, he worked at a shop called The Bookman and developed his lifelong enthusiasm for book collecting. In 1964–1965 he was awarded a Guggenheim fellowship for creative writing. In 1969, McMurtry moved to the vicinity of Washington, D. C., and together with two partners started a bookshop in Georgetown, which he named Booked Up. Later in 1988 he opened another branch of the store in his hometown of Archer City, next to the Royal Theatre, which he immortalized in *The Last Picture Show*. Because of economic pressures, McMurtry decided in 2012 to sell the bulk of his inventory, retaining only a portion to maintain the store. On April 29, 2011, McMurtry married Norma Faye Kesey, the widow of Ken Kesey, on April 29, in a civil ceremony in Archer City.

Throughout his career, the settings of McMurtry's novels have rotated among the frontier, the ranch, the small town, and the city, with most of them set in Texas but some in Hollywood, Washington, Las Vegas, or elsewhere. He admits to being somewhat conflicted by an attraction and a repulsion to all of these locales. His early novels, *Horseman, Pass By* (1961) and *Leaving Cheyenne* (1963), are set on ranches and farms and deal with the historical transformation McMurtry experienced in his childhood. The Thalia novels fictionalize Archer City and explore the intricacies and intimacies of small-town life, and many other works, including *Moving On* (1970) and *Terms of Endearment* (1977), are set in Houston and Dallas and portray in detail human relationships and their complexities in the modern city and suburb . His well-known *Lonesome Dove* saga, which includes *Lonesome Dove* (1986), which won the Pulitzer Prize, *Streets of Laredo* (1993), *Dead Man's Walk* (1995), and *Comanche Moon* (1997), consists of historical romances set in the late nineteenth century in the wake of the Comanche wars and in the midst of the cattle kingdoms. This variation in time and place is mirrored in his own life. When McMurtry left Texas and moved to Northern Virginia, he resided there for nearly a decade. During the 1980s he lived in an apartment over his bookstore, but he kept apartments in Arizona, California, and Washington. After the success of *Lonesome Dove*, when he returned permanently to Archer City and opened Booked Up, his hometown honored him with "Larry McMurtry Day," and he attended and even spoke. Many of his popular and critically acclaimed novels have been adapted into film for screen and television, including *Horseman, Pass By* as *Hud* (Martin Ritt, 1963, three Academy Awards), *The Last Picture Show* (Peter Bogdanovich, 1971, two Academy Awards), *Terms of Endearment* (James L. Brooks, 1983, five Academy Awards), and *Lonesome Dove* (Simon Wincer, 1989), which won seven Emmy Awards and remains perhaps the most popular and respected miniseries in the history of the genre. Among his many accomplishments and activities, he has served as president of the PEN American Center, which promotes writers' freedom of expression; in that capacity he organized support for Salman Rushdie after the Ayatollah Khomeini issued his fatwa against the writer. Thus, in his life and work, Larry McMurtry has immersed himself in the human scene. His work demonstrates an intense preoccupation with the past, its character and richness, and its living reality in the present moment.

Overview, Influence, Character, and the Novel Form

In coming to terms with the largest cross section of McMurtry's works, readers and critics confront a common conundrum, even a prejudice. He is among the most popular novelists of his time, and he is popular in a distinctively modern way. Not only have his novels sold millions of copies, appealing to a broad base of readers, but also from the beginning his work has been adapted into films, beginning with *Horseman, Pass By,* which became *Hud* in 1963 and starred the already famous Paul Newman. His novels lack the surface-level complexity of the work of the high modernists and of many contemporary authors who employ techniques and aesthetics similar to those of the moderns. His works are readable and often quite entertaining, but they make a different set of demands, sometimes vexing critics, who react with confusion to his complex and sometimes purposefully directionless plots. Still, while certain serious and acclaimed writers of the time appeal to a more limited audience, McMurtry has been widely read from his first work on.

Much to his own dismay, his later Westerns appealed to those who extol the myth of the West and the Western cowboy, though a careful observation of both the novels and the films reveals a strong revisionist sensibility and a firm challenge to the myth. In his early novels, there is a quality of whimsy and the appeal of love and romance, in works ranging from *Leaving Cheyenne* through the later narratives set in Thalia. These aspects of appeal are intimately linked to themes of transience and loss of place. Most have proven remarkably cinematic, and, judging from the popular success of the adaptations, there seems to be something inherent in McMurtry's work that translates to cinema with an ease quite rare among novels. There is a host of possible reasons for this, but perhaps the most obvious are McMurtry's remarkable skill with character and dialogue and his frequent involvement with the adaptations themselves. Often, the same vision that motivates the novel motivates the adaptation, and when it doesn't, the characters are commonly so rich and interesting that "faithful" adaptation becomes a driving motivation of the screenwriters. It is tempting to conclude that McMurtry lacks the overt preoccupation with literary style typical of his immediate forebears William Faulkner, Ernest Hemingway, and, perhaps most notably, his rough contemporary Cormac McCarthy. But close scrutiny of sentences and paragraphs reveals not only an identifiable style but a distinctive mood and flavor uniquely McMurtry's own. Much of this is difficult to capture in a stylistic analysis, but it is very much a feature of tone. An excerpt from *Terms of Endearment* (1975) will serve as an example. General Scott is one of the main character Aurora Greenway's many suitors, and he is well deserving of attention given his successes in life, but Aurora is playfully unimpressed, and she sends the General into fits of frustration.:

> In his prime he had commanded a tank division, and attempts to get through to Aurora almost always brought his tanks to mind. He had even begun to dream of tanks, for the first time since the war. Only a few nights

before he had had a very happy dream in which he had driven up River Oaks Boulevard standing in the turret of his largest tank. The people in the country club at the end of the boulevard had all come out and lined up and looked at him respectfully. . . . General Scott had many dreams involving tanks, many of which ended with him crunching through the lower walls of Aurora's house, into her living room, or sometimes her kitchen. (101)

There is a playfulness and whimsy to the prose and the situation constructed, and there are many scenes of this sort in McMurtry's work. Humor abounds, but beneath the humor and very much implicated in it is human frustration in many forms, in this case a man's frustration at a woman's willful ambivalence. There is even a conversational, oral quality to the language, and McMurtry is perhaps drawing from the tradition of conversation and storytelling so common in his region. The conversational quality and humor belie the underlying seriousness of situations involving human beings oddly and frequently on the verge of choiceless despair. Still, whatever literary characteristics might emerge from style and language have not (as in the case of other authors) limited his readership or intimidated filmmakers interested in successful story material. On the contrary, major directors and studios have been eager to adapt his work, contributing greatly to his fame, popularity, and general reception in the print media. But even in his Westerns set in the nineteenth century, there is nothing formulaic about his plots and characters. His storylines are frequently unpredictable, his situations stark and unsentimental, his characters often endearing but complex and deeply flawed. It is interesting to note that, given the success of the miniseries adaptation of *Lonesome Dove*, the television studios could not resist adapting the entire series, from the prequel *Dead Man's Walk* (1995; miniseries 1996) to the sequels *Streets of Laredo* (1993; miniseries 1995) and *Comanche Moon* (1997; miniseries 2008). But they could also not resist creating their own alternative film sequel, *Return to Lonesome Dove* (1993), significantly altering the plot, sentimentalizing situations and especially characters, and reaffirming the myth of the West in ways McMurtry did not intend. Thus, there is something immediately appealing about Larry McMurtry's work, and the principal challenge for the critical reader is how to read it carefully enough to move beyond the surface appeal, beyond the veneer of romance in the case of the Westerns and the pleasing nostalgia in the early novels.

It is worth remembering that McMurtry is among the most highly trained and well-read authors in American literary history, possessing an undergraduate degree in literature, an M.A. in creative writing, and a Stegner fellowship in creative writing. He has absorbed the tradition of the novel deeply and intensely, and he demonstrates that interest in his many epigraphs to canonical

authors before and within his novels. He stands, then, at the end of a long line
of authors who both were remarkably popular in their own time and emerged
later as important figures in a literary tradition: Cooper, Austen, Thackeray,
Dickens, London, Dreiser, Hemingway, as well as Henry James and D. H.
Lawrence, the latter two from whom McMurtry took the name he gave his
son, James Lawrence McMurtry. Consistent with our best understanding of
the novel form, a successful reading of Larry McMurtry's novels must involve
a reading practice attentive to what is valuable in his forebears: language and
style, yes, but also the sometimes deceptive complexity and unpredictability
of characters, universal in nature but situated firmly in time and place. Comprehending the importance of McMurtry's work does in fact require this at-
tentiveness to the complexities of genre, as well as a recognition of his deep
understanding of the form, his varied use of subgenres, and his frequent and
creative combination of them.

Readers who admire McMurtry might conceivably be confronted with a
simple question: Which McMurtry do you prefer? Many of his novels might be
conceived, in a term used by Graham Greene to describe his own work, as "en-
tertainments," novels designed for readability and surface-level appeal and not
intended to be scrutinized rigorously. These might include *Somebody's Darling*
(1978), *Cadillac Jack* (1982), and *The Desert Rose* (1983), though some of these
works deserve some attention for their presentation of his common themes. But
among his many serious inquiries into the human condition, do you prefer the
McMurtry of *Lonesome Dove*, of *The Last Picture Show*, or of *Moving On*?
Although close reading reveals certain continuities in these works, such as the
Texas setting, the preoccupation with the effects of change upon individuals
and relationships, and the intricate and endearing flaws and limitations of
people, there are significant differences as well. As such, it becomes important to chart the thematic preoccupations in these various works and periods,
particularly as they relate to the subgenres McMurtry so deftly employs and
blends. The earliest novels, *Horseman, Pass By* and *Leaving Cheyenne,* are set
in the twentieth century, in a time by no means remote from the author's own.
They deal with rural and semirural settings and the waning ranch culture and
its complex transformation into oil culture. They do not particularly qualify
as historical romances in the tradition of Sir Walter Scott and James Fenimore
Cooper, as do the Westerns of the *Lonesome Dove* saga or other Westerns
such as *Anything for Billy* (1989) and *Buffalo Girls* (1990). But in terms of
theme these early novels respond to many of the same concerns. Nineteenth-
century historical romances, which derived their form from the works of Sir
Walter Scott's Waverley novels, are overtly mythical in nature. From the Filsen
narratives that portrayed the exploits of Daniel Boone, the Revolutionary War

novels of William Gilmore Simms, to, most notably, James Fenimore Cooper's *The Leatherstocking Tales*, this subgenre of the novel began to constitute an American national mythology, with characters that were larger than life and emblematic of the emerging nation's values, self-perceptions, aspirations, and ambitions. Central to these works was historical change itself, which in a kind of sweeping dialectic involved the competing impulses of progress and reaction. In the best historical romances, there is a painful ambivalence that creates powerful tensions that lead to deeply moving narratives. Character are caught in a sweeping process of historical transformation that is not wholly positive or negative, as the forces of modern modes of social organization and new economies improve the world in many ways but displace premodern lives and communities in the process. Always imbued with an epic and subtly tragic sense of inevitability, people are caught in a historical dynamic they do not understand, as time itself with a kind of immaterial power alters the social scene and, with it, the inner reality of human identity.

Frontiersmen are simultaneously and perhaps ironically the icons of the past, born of the land, united with its natural processes, and acclimated to its brutish laws, but they also represent the vanguard of civilization, bringing Euro-American culture into the vast and untamed wilderness. These new heroes become tragic witness to a process they themselves initiate, and they frequently lament the passing of a frontier in its twilight. Ironically, these heroes are the mythic representation of values still prized by those who read about them and respond to them, but a careful understanding of their role in history must lead to a more vexed response. They possess virtues that only partly remain relevant. They are figures tragically out of time and agents of a change they cannot anticipate. These same concerns are present in the twentieth century, and Texas is one locale in which they are experienced acutely. In *Horseman, Pass By,* the open land and the cattle range, often governed by the same mythically constituted values of the frontier hero, give way to industrial civilization in the form of the oil industry. This tension is directly represented in the conflict between the old man Homer Bannon and his stepson Hud, one representing older ranch culture and a set of values built on creating and sustaining a tangible product, the other linked to a more malevolent system of economic value built largely on monetary exchange, with the grandson as observer. In *Leaving Cheyenne,* Gideon Fry and his friend Johnny remain close throughout their lifetime, but Gid, though a rancher, is also the proto-capitalist preoccupied with acquisition, while Johnny remains dedicated to a freedom that is possible precisely because he seeks to own nothing. Both manifest heroic virtues, both emerge from the range, but in a sense the tension embodied in the frontier hero is divided between them, one man wedded to progress and the other to reaction. In Gid's case, his commitment is to the principle of owner-ship and to the land, values that can be seen in his father, from whom he inher-ited his impulse to acquisition and work ethic: "Dad had about ten thousand acres; he had the whole country to pick from and he picked careful. There was a creek to the southeast and a creek to the northwest, and the River down the middle, so if there was water anywhere in the country, we had it. And of course he had built good tanks" (127).

Gid has a strong appreciation for the landscape at an aesthetic and personal level, but he has a tremendous respect for his father's practicality and learned sense of the material value of a particular piece of land. Much like Homer Bannon, Gid and his father are committed to an ethic of productivity, but for them, unlike Johnny, work is not enough. Gid and his father must tame the land and make it serve. It is an ethic not without its merits and its problems, embodying the fundamental problematic of modernity, its value in creating the greatest material good for the most people and its destructive potential in the decimation of the natural. Even in the novels set just before and after McMur-try's birth, history and historical process become an important theme, as the narratives contend with the way in which social and economic forces bear upon the personal circumstances of the characters and the nature of their evolving identities. The beauty and the relevance of these early novels lie in part in the manner in which the individual identities of characters and the traumas related to them are integrated into larger social and historical themes. Individual identity and historical process are intimately co-implicated. History is nothing without the human beings who initiate and embody it, and people become the unwitting chaff that history buffets, ignores, or disregards.

The Western genre echoes in these early works and later in the Thalia nov-els, as landscape and the figures of the cowboy and rancher remain central. It is not surprising, then, that McMurtry would be drawn to the genre directly. Though he achieved both popularity and acclaim for many of his works writ-ten in the 1960s and 1970s, that fame grew exponentially with the publication of *Lonesome Dove* and its subsequent prequel and sequels. This very popular-ity, enhanced significantly by the various miniseries, tends to obscure the com-plexity of McMurtry's relationship to the West and the Western. Both the first novel and the film were quite inappropriately read as unvarnished celebrations of the Western genre in its most popular, mythic, and nationalist form. A care-ful reading of *Lonesome Dove*, and particularly *Streets of Laredo* and *Dead Man's Walk*, reveals McMurtry's critical inquiry into the values that inform the genre from its inception. In fact, he is quite forthright in his criticism of the Western myth and its central hero. In an interview in 1988 with Mervyn Roth-stein of the *New York Times*, published three years after *Lonesome Dove* was published and just before the airing of the miniseries, McMurtry clarified his attitude toward the Western. He said, "I'm a critic of the myth of the cowboy. . . . I don't feel that it's a myth that pertains, and since it's a part of my heritage I feel it's a legitimate task to criticize it."[2] He went on to account for his attitude by drawing a distinction between the myth and actual history, reflecting his significant reading on the subject: "If you actually read the biography of any of the famous gunfighters . . . they led very drab, mostly very repetitive, not very exciting lives." From his novels, it is clear that McMurtry understands the importance of the Western as a mythology in the collective American consciousness, and ultimately his approach is to embody and scrutinize the myth and to reconstitute it in more complex terms, rather than merely discard it. The interview reflects a quiet frustration with the tendency of readers to see *Lonesome Dove* in unvarnished mythic terms, and it is important to place any reading of McMurtry's Westerns in the context of his deep understanding of the genre itself.

Drawing certainly from the frontier romances of the early nineteenth century, the Western as an identifiable genre came into being with the "dime novels" that mythologized actual as well as wholly fictional cowboys and gunfighters. They first appeared in 1860, when Erasmus Beadle, having moved from James Fenimore Cooper's home county near Lake Otsego, New York, established a publishing empire in New York City that appealed to a mass audience. Beginning with songbooks and handbooks priced at ten cents, he began a weekly series of orange-backed dime novels, primarily set on the Western frontier. In actuality they weren't novels, since few of them exceeded thirty thousand words. The demand for these tracts was overwhelming, and the original print runs of sixty thousand were followed by multiple reprints. Edward S. Ellis's *Seth Jones,* number eight in the original series, sold more than four hundred thousand copies, and between 1855 and 1860 Beadle's total sales approached five million copies. Fictional characters such as Deadwood Dick emerged, and actual frontiersmen such as Wild Bill Hickok (James Butler Hickok), Buffalo Bill (William Frederick Cody), and Calamity Jane (Martha Jane Canary), as well as outlaws and gunmen such as Billy the Kid (William Bonny), became the raw material for rather cheap and formulaic hero types. Even this most superficial of genres began to reveal some of the tensions and values that informed the Western experience, and characters evolved in sequels, often emerging as violent, self-serving, and morally ambiguous.[3] Of course, given their enormous popularity, these dime novels entered the age of film, becoming one of the most popular and resilient cinema genres of the twentieth century.

In this context it is important to note that the genre is highly variegated, taking on both affirmative and revisionist attitudes toward the Western hero.

Proliferating in the 1930s in the form of B Westerns, they developed into the more complex narratives of Howard Hawkes, John Ford, Sergio Leone, Sam Peckinpah, and Clint Eastwood, all of which explore the frontier experience in the rich context of history, frequently functioning as allegories of contemporaneous historical circumstances such as the Cold War and the Vietnam era. In fact, a remarkable shift in Western films occurred in the late 1960s, a change that led to many Westerns that were remarkably different in form and thematic content from those that had come before. Emphasizing the role of contemporary myth in reflecting the ideological conflicts of a given historical moment, Richard Slotkin linked a noticeable transformation in the Western to the deep social crises that occurred as a result of the Vietnam War. In the early 1970s, as the war was coming to its tragic conclusion, a new, "alternative" Western emerged. Anticipated certainly by the "spaghetti Westerns" of Sergio Leone, this genre took on a number of forms, all of which contradict in various ways the assumed moral stature of the American hero and demonstrate a willingness to confront violence more directly.[4]

Like these filmmakers, McMurtry, as well as other late practitioners of the Western genre in novels and film, was noticeably interested not only in reconsidering or criticizing the myth but also in exploring in a self-reflexive manner the nature and origin of the genre itself. In the Academy Award–winning film *Unforgiven* (1992), director Clint Eastwood and screenwriter David Webb Peoples deliberately called attention to their film as fiction, fable, and myth. The first scene begins with a scrolling written introduction to the "story" of the gunfighter William Munny. Written in the ornate style of the nineteenth century, the story begins and ends with this language, calling attention to the fable-like quality of the character himself and the dubious and questionable reality of the events that unfold on the screen. As the story continues, a dime novelist emerges as a character, perhaps even the writer of the fable itself. He is weak, dishonest, gullible, and, most important, a poor writer. It is clear that he will tell the story not just of Munny himself but of the many other raw, unethical, and violent characters that became the substance of the false myth of the Western.

In this and other films, the Western genre is scrutinized and reconceptualized. It remains a potent story pattern, still resonating, as all myths do, with the values and issues central to the nation's complex history of expansion and settlement. The Western is the American morality play. It is the most common genre through which American culture constitutes, considers, dismantles, and reconstitutes its fundamental values, all in the rich context of personal and social frames of ethical reference. As such, the genre possesses the potential both to reaffirm and to aggressively re-adapt American mythological conception. It is precisely this genre potential that McMurtry recognizes in all his Westerns, clearly with greater subtlety in *Lonesome Dove* and more openly in *Streets of Laredo* and *Dead Man's Walk,* which are darker and more open in their impulse to demythologize. In these novels, the Western hero appears in quite appealing terms, but he is portrayed, through McCrae and Call, with a certain multiplicity, as each character both embodies and responds to the myth in sometimes quite conscious ways. This awareness of genre and fictionality becomes clear later in *Anything for Billy,* where McMurtry tells the story of William Bonny ("Billy the Kid"), one of main characters in the dime novels. In this work, McMurtry, like Eastwood and Peoples, makes the dime novelist the central character, comically emphasizing his falsehood and lack of literary skill and perception. The dime novelist narrator is antiheroic and self-deprecating, and his motive for creating Westerns, principally boredom, is portrayed as comic and deeply pathetic.

> I doubt anyone has caught a worse case of dime-novel mania than I had. First I read them, then I had to try writing them. The fever they aroused in me was a kind of mental malaria. Even now, with all the characters in the story long since dead . . . occasionally the old fever flares up again.
>
> I had been a Philadelphia gentleman, reasonably attentive to the duties of my station; but in a matter of months I became wholly distracted, descending each morning into a sea of daughters with prairies in my head. (16–17)

A gentleman of presumed education and cultivation Ben Sippy may be, but he is still susceptible to the allure of the emerging American mythology, so much so that he becomes a perpetuator. It is frankly quite interesting that McMurtry decided to demonstrate how the myth itself is perpetuated from a consciousness that is in many ways unconscious of its own addiction to the myth, and Sippy gains a degree of self-reflection only after traveling west and meeting Billy Bone. Sippy is an interesting character and tremendously important in understanding McMurtry's notion of the role of storytelling as it relates to the Western. For him, Westerns are tall tales, full of intended and unintended humor, containing truths but far from true. Thus, McMurtry's Westerns must be read with firm attention to the author's own declared antipathy to the myth, expressed not with a simple realism but with the potency of imaginative storytelling, informed by a legitimate basis in genuine history and the violent actuality that underlies it.

McMurtry's understanding of the novel form is demonstrated by the skill with which he effectively enacts it. Readers are tempted to leave questions of genre at bay because his plots often engage quickly and his characters often take on an immediate familiarity and sympathy. But it is clear that McMurtry quite self-consciously employs and reconceptualizes the historical romance, and he does so with other subgenres as well, most particularly the novel of manners. Of course, this form is broad in scope, but it can be defined with some degree of precision, and its history can be reasonably charted. There are a number of characteristics that typify the novel of manners. First, it emerged primarily in England in the late eighteenth and early nineteenth centuries, in the context of a dense and socially variegated British culture. Its primary subject is people in society, functioning and often struggling as complex psychological beings, in a world defined by recognizable conventions of behavior, manners, mores, and even preconceived social values. Individual examples of the novel of manners are frequently detailed in historical texture, always located in time and place. Its earliest practitioners date to the birth of the novel in the eighteenth century and include Henry Fielding (1707–1754), as well as Samuel Richardson (1689–1761). Perhaps the most popular and enduring novelist in this tradition is Jane Austen (1775–1817), and elements of this genre are present in the work of William Makepeace Thackeray (1811–1863), Mary Anne Evans (George Eliot: 1819–1880), and, of course, Charles Dickens (1812–1870). Although the form certainly evolved, it may be argued that later examples can be found in the works of Henry James (1843–1916), Sinclair Lewis (1885–1951), and F. Scott Fitzgerald (1896–1940).[5] What typifies the novel of manners is character and character relations, and McMurtry's particular contribution is his willingness to sacrifice virtually anything to the portrayal of character within a dense social context, even relinquishing quite often tightly structured plots. For McMurtry, the proper portrayal of characters in social realism involves the same lack of resolution and order that life itself involves.

Some of the same tensions present in the historical romance also inform the novel of manners, particularly the malleability of social classes in the industrial and postindustrial age. In this historical period, classes existed and were defined by social practices and "manners," but they shifted and changed as economic realities defined and redefined the contours of social stratification. The novel of manners takes as its focus the interactions of various groups in dense social contexts, if not in the city then certainly in the textured societies of the British and American aristocracies—in country manor houses and on wealthy estates. In contrast to those used for historical romances, these settings are intentionally ordinary and recognizable, and plots are by and large plausible if at times a bit neat in terms of appealing outcomes. The purpose of the novel of manners at its best is to render characters as complex, psychologically dynamic, and real but also to demonstrate that these interior complexities bear upon and must interact with a social reality. With respect to marriage, the claims of love must meet the claims of class convention. The desires of the heart are compromised by the compulsion for wealth and social position. The need to express openly confronts the limitations of propriety. All of these conflicts are the primary subject of the novel of manners.

It has often been noted that, at least in the nineteenth century, the social novel was less suited to American settings. In *The American Novel and Its Tradition* (1957), Richard Chase went so far as to distinguish the American tradition from the British, associating the American novel with the "romance" and the British novel with the socially textured novel of manners. Chase's distinction was extremely influential and, later, somewhat controversial, but the general consensus is that it remains valid at least as a way of meaningfully partitioning American and British novels of the nineteenth century.[6] The central claim that American culture originally lacked the dense social texture necessary to allow for the novel of manners, however, clearly breaks down for the twentieth century, in the wake of the industrial revolution and the process of urbanization. In this context, many of Larry McMurtry's novels represent a late-twentieth-century manifestation of the novel of manners; they are distinctive in their radical extension of the social realism that occurs frequently through plot resolutions typical of the genre in earlier eras.

It is tempting to notice more immediately the time-specific social conventions of the nineteenth-century British parlor: the styles of dress, the formal etiquette, the ornate speech in public settings, the bows and curtsies. But careful scrutiny of many of McMurtry's urban novels reveals the central concerns present in the novel of manners. The social reality he creates in works such as *Moving On* (1970), *All My Friends Are Going to Be Strangers* (1972), and *Terms of Endearment* (1975) involves the rich intricacies of character relations firmly grounded in Houston. Texas remains in large part McMurtry's world, but it is now a Texas emblematic of the American city and the American suburb. *Moving On* focuses on the life of Patsy Carpenter, a young married woman in Houston, and the novel renders place in all its cultural complexity as it focuses on the interaction of the rural and the urban, with rodeo riders, urban sophisticates, and Hollywood characters, the latter providing a certain color and comic mood to the setting. In *All My Friends Are Going to Be Strangers,* McMurtry fictionalizes elements of his own experience as a young successful Texas writer wanders back and forth from California to Texas, attempting to sort out the densities of the social world and his place within it as a writer and as a human being. In *Terms of Endearment,* McMurtry portrays a phenomenon quite typical of Americans: migration as a middle-aged New England widow, Aurora Greenway, moves to Houston, raises a daughter, and in the end must deal with her child's marital troubles and untimely death. The intimacies of these relations, the terms that endear, must be discovered in the context of movement from one city setting to another, from one relationship to another. In this sense, the novel of manners provides a set of thematic concerns that McMurtry explores anew in modern Texas, which is a place that offers its own social and cultural densities, as recognizably human concerns—self-discovery, the pursuit of love and intimacy, the desire for home—negotiate with a textured and ever-changing world.

Thus, in the context of many of his contemporaries and immediate fore-bears in American literature and the literature of the American West—Wallace Stegner, Edward Abbey, Cormac McCarthy, Philip Roth, Don DeLillo, and Toni Morrison—Larry McMurtry offers a compelling and distinctive contribution. Varying in locale but rooted in the West, his works demonstrate that he is quite clearly a writer of place and time. But he is by no means a mere regionalist, since his works delve with force and immediacy into the soul of character, into human situations enriched by the details that only region can provide but that embody the universal. His novels contend with the irrevocable contingencies of time as it threads its way through individual lives, weaving out of them the grand tapestry of his region and the nation.

CHAPTER 2

The Early Works

Larry McMurtry left his hometown of Archer City in 1954, entering college for a short time at Rice University and finishing at North Texas State College in Denton. In this first of many moves, McMurtry didn't venture far. In Houston, in his late teens, Rice seemed perhaps too far away, though with playful chagrin he mainly mentioned his inability to comprehend the college math course. But the sweep and breadth of the large urban campus seems to have changed him, and the immense university library was an invigorating contrast to the provincial world he had known. He embraced literature with a passion at North Texas, both as a student and as an emerging young writer, and even as an undergraduate he demonstrated a tremendous capacity for work and a commitment to craft. He wrote and later burned fifty-two apprentice short stories, but in them he already understood that the home he had left was stuff enough for volumes. It took William Faulkner some time to discover his "postage stamp of native soil." McMurtry held Archer City to heart from the beginning.

In these early works and in his first two published novels, the confluence of past and present, the almost inexpressible anguish of transience, are the felt substance of experience and memory, which as they come to life in descriptions of landscape can barely be distinguished. The ranches and their industrious owners, freedom-loving cowboys, wealth hungry proto-capitalists, twilight skylines silhouetted in mechanical horseheads that lifted black oil from the open range—these are things McMurtry took as emblems of twentieth-century America. In this sense, McMurtry is one of only a few authors who establish and develop region in this manner, as a grand metaphor for a national and even transnational phenomenon we call modernity. The West had become iconic in a national mythology that had gained international import, and its essence was wildness, in the land and in the men and women who occupied it. That wildness signified the preindustrial and the premodern. The modern West as born in reality and portrayed in McMurtry's novels becomes an effective region to chart the contrast between old and new. McMurtry wrote two early stories, one about the destruction of a cattle herd by disease and another about an aging cattleman's funeral. He decided to connect them and to develop them into a novel. He sent the manuscript to the *Texas Quarterly* in the hope that it would publish part of his work as a supplement, and Frank Wardlaw read the novel and sent it to an acquaintance at Harper Brothers in New York. Harper's decided to publish it as *Horseman, Pass By* (1961). In the 1960s, McMurtry was clearly comfortable in the academic world, teaching at Texas Christian University in Fort Worth and later at Rice, all the while writing some of his earliest and most enduring novels, beginning with *Leaving Cheyenne* (1963). These early works display what would become a pervasive concern with human relationships comically and tragically rendered: with love and intimacy between men and women, with friendship among men and across genders, often emerging in endearing if peculiar personal arrangements that avoid conventional patterns of permanence, even as they painfully seek them. These early novels, then, are straightforward and poignant expressions of themes McMurtry would further develop throughout his long career, themes that reflect contemporary concerns about the instability of relationships and communities, even as those relationships and communities are portrayed as deeply and incalculably valuable.

Horseman, Pass By (1961)

McMurtry's first novel, *Horseman, Pass By*, takes its title from William Butler Yeats poem, "Under Ben Bulben," the last three lines of which are "Cast a cold eye / on life, on death / Horseman, pass by." This allusion suggests the sense of conflict and transience the novel captures so vividly. There is an ambiguity to the allusion, especially when it is considered in the context of the novel itself. In starkly naturalistic terms, one must recognize life's indifference and the ever-present reality of death. But the novel blends this indifference with a number of human relationships and heartfelt associations that qualify the harshness of the changing world the characters must face. The world, in this case rural Texas, is simultaneously beautiful and emblematic of loss, the source of comedy and tragedy, joy and pain. *Horseman, Pass By* received generally positive reviews, and critics almost immediately recognized McMurtry as a powerful new voice in American letters. Noted especially for his skill at storytelling and his wistful portrayal of America in a perpetual state of change, he created a degree of genuine excitement by his first significant publication. Reviews registered a basic understanding of the novel's themes and a general grasp of the subgenre

McMurtry evoked most clearly—the American historical romance, with its central tensions of progress and reaction.[1]

The novel was quickly adapted into film as *Hud*, directed by Martin Ritt and starring Paul Newman in the title role, with Patricia Neal as the housekeeper, Halmea. The script held largely to the novel regarding the theme of transition, though it altered some of the relationships. Hud becomes the son rather than the stepson of Homer Bannon, and, though he is depicted as brutal and insensitive, his more unpleasant traits are mitigated perhaps by a complicated relationship to his father reminiscent of the one portrayed in Steinbeck's *East of Eden*. Newman's performance ever so slightly recalls James Dean's in the film adaptation of that Steinbeck novel. The most interesting deviation is the casting of Patricia Neal. In the novel, the narrator, Lonnie, and Hud are attracted to the middle-aged Halmea, who is African American. In portraying these sexual tensions, the film deliberately avoids the race issue, a choice perhaps understandable given the time but interesting nevertheless. The novel portrays Halmea as caring tremendously for Lonnie but also aware of his emerging sexuality and his attraction to her. She is worldly, experienced, and by no means put off by his innocent desires. At the same time, Lonnie, perhaps in contrast to Hud, sees beyond race and is virtually blind to it in his fundamental respect and attraction to Halmea. It is perhaps the sexual dimension to her character that led the filmmakers to avoid casting an African American, since dealing with interracial attraction might have attracted undue attention and controversy.

The novel avoids none of these complications. From the beginning of his career McMurtry addressed social issues often considered controversial: race, sexuality, gender tensions, and unflinching brutality and violence. From the opening frame of the novel, landscape emerges if not as character certainly as a player in a grand drama in which human beings exhibit their best and worst qualities as they negotiate the reality of historical change. *Horseman, Pass By* is acutely aware of its antecedents: Cooper's *The Leatherstocking Tales* (1827–1841), William Gilmore Simms's *The Yemassee* (1844), and the already developed Western genre in all its misunderstood complexity. Though brief and remarkably controlled, the novel has an epic quality typical of others set on the American frontier, as human beings contend with nature itself in all its beauty and breadth, its sublimity and awesome grandeur. Texas is the locale, but America is the subject, and the novel derives its power from an inherent faith in the humble dignity of human beings who possess an irrepressible capacity to dream and imagine, even in the face of historical forces that circumscribe the choices made. The story is told from the point of view of Lonnie Bannon, grandson of Homer Bannon, an aging rancher who is in many ways inseparable from the range he owns. Lonnie's waking dream life is clear from the beginning:

I went to my room, but it was a long time that night before I went to sleep. I read a little of *From Here to Eternity,* and then lay on my bed wide awake in the darkness, my head full of old sights and half dreams, some nice and some uneasy. I remembered something Hud had told me once about my daddy: how he had killed my real grandmother. Hud said a snake had crawled up on the cellar, and Daddy shot at it and the bullet ricocheted off and hit grandmother in the head. Granddad was off in the pasture, and she died under the sycamore tree before he got home. I never had the nerve to ask grandad about it. But I knew that the ranch wasn't as cheerful as it had been. (69)

Lonnie seems to have a distinctive capacity to dream and ponder not only in imagistic but intellectual terms, and this capacity seems central to him as an emerging hero in a changing land. His other dreams comprehend the totality of Texas in its most pristine state, but they also comprehend the changes that have transformed it, the ranches and the horses and, in the present, the highways that transport people away and back again. In this reflection, he remains closer to home, considering the tragic and sometimes unpredictable circumstances that condition his life, the events that brought Hud into his world, and the tragedy from which his father perhaps never fully recovered. These dreams and reflections are both expansive and particular, and all people in some form share that kind of experience. But Lonnie seems particularly prone to ponder, reflect, and dream.

As the novel begins, it is clear that Homer and Lonnie live with Homer's second wife and his stepson, Hud, a self-serving and angry young man who sees the world very differently from Homer. In a certain way, the moral center of the novel is Halmea, middle aged and attractive, who draws the sexual attention of Lonnie and the more pernicious advances of the older Hud. As the story begins, Homer discovers that one of his cattle has died mysteriously, and over time he learns that his herd is infected with foot and mouth disease, perhaps from exposure to some Mexican cattle Homer has purchased. As the family members contend with the potential destruction of their ranch, they must consider how they will negotiate the future, and this problem crystallizes in a conflict between Homer, who clings to the older ranching life and rejects the idea of entering the oil economy, and Hud, who embraces the opportunity for wealth at the expense of any higher motives or moral vision. The young Lonnie is witness to this dramatic tension and must try to comprehend it even as he struggles with growing up, grappling with his own hopes and the intensity of his own half-understood desires. Lonnie then becomes a kind of hero in the making, influenced certainly by the past but drawn to the future. His is a coming of age that parallels the transformation of his region and nation, and his tendency to ponder and dream, reflects the same tendency often associated with America itself. In that sense, that age-old theme of the American dream, its beauty and its tentative successes and failures, informs *Horseman, Pass By* in the deepest and clearest sense. Hope, promise, and undefined desire, together with avaricious greed and want, are at the core of the national experience, in this case centered in a state that functions as an emblem of the nation.

The novel consists of fourteen chapters of medium length divided into subchapters that vary in number. All are told from a conventional first-person point of view, and though the dialogue is written in a comprehensible but marked regional dialect, the exposition and description are for the most part in Standard English, though occasionally a regional expression appears, reminding readers that Lonnie is the teller of the tale. These segments are framed, however, with a prologue and an epilogue in italics, both of which work to emphasize that the entire story itself is imbued with the personal memory and individual preoccupations of the teller. There is a fable-like quality to these frames, colored with the ghostly, immaterial, dream-haunted aura of wistful and even tortured recollection. What haunts and compels is the land itself, which becomes apparent from the opening sentences:

> I remember how green the early oat fields were, that year, and how the plains looked in April, after the mesquite leafed out. Spring had come dry for seven straight years, and Granddad and the other cattlemen in Dry Bean County had had to watch the bare spots widening in their pastures. . . . When I rode out with him on Saturdays, Granddad would sometimes get down from his horse, to show me how the grass was shooting its runners over the doughty ground; and he told me that nature would always work her own cures, if people would be patient enough, and give her time. (3)

Nostalgia and recollection emerge from the opening sentence as energetic forces that will animate the reader's perception of the land. But it is a recognition deeply informed by experience, infused as it is written with the vivid details of a nature that is full of life. Much like Willa Cather does in *My Antonia* as she describes Nebraska, McMurtry takes rural Texas, what many see as a wasted landscape, and transforms it through a vision that is both minute and expansive, as the particulars of the land and the life that occupy it are rendered specifically, building into a rich interior vision brought to the reader in memory and in words. McMurtry's artistic challenge, taken and met, is to transform a landscape normally seen as barren and, through accurate description and visionary precision, to render it anew. Characters such as Homer Bannon and later Lonnie Bannon have always viewed the land not only as beautiful but also as a life-sustaining source of transcendent meaning. The description blends a kind of epic sweep with vivid imagery, from the "green" of the oat fields with "leafed out" mesquite, the "dry spots" in parched pastures, to the even greater detail of "the grass . . . shooting its runners over the doughty ground." The passage sacrifices the wider vision of an open range in favor of particulars but never seems to, since with a peculiar narrative sleight of hand the sense of breadth so typical of Western landscape is preserved, through the evocative use of certain words, names, clauses, and phrases. "Spring had come dry," "Grand-dad and the other cattlemen," "Dry Bean County," "When I rode out with him on Saturdays"—these are expressions flavored with the visual iconography of the American West, and they inevitably call to mind the epic sweep of the region both in fact and in American cultural memory. Drought, the old rancher and the cowboy, the oddly poetic intensity of the county's name, the image of a young man riding the range with a seasoned veteran—all these things come together in painterly fashion. Blended with particular images, they achieve a deceptively intricate and appealing texture, and the crescendo is as American as can be, as the older wise man of the land tells the boy that "nature would always work her own cures, if people would be patient enough, and give her time." It is an insight accurate and practical yet romantic, recalling Emersonian and Thoreauvian concepts of natural beauty, integrity, sustenance, and implied spiritual rejuvenation.

Described in italics as a pure recollection displaced from the current moment, this visionary landscape captures a reality deeper than present perception, presenting the land as more than possession but also as a source of identity and brotherhood that must be respected even as those who tend it alter it permanently. This paradoxical blend of respect and exploitation lifts the description beyond a simplistic and highly romanticized worship of nature. The figures of the rancher and the cowboy are ideal to capture this paradox. They have altered the original grasslands into cattle ranges and are the immediate beneficiaries of the displacement of the Native Americans and the slaughter of the American bison. But they stand against the more modern capitalistic exploitation of Eastern financial interests and the even more destructive forces of the oil industry. In this initial description, McMurtry explores these ironies, which become the substance of character conflict in the main narrative of the novel. Though these tensions are rooted in history and though the novel is informed by the tradition of the American historical romance, these characters are portrayed in vividly realistic terms. They possess a mythic quality in that they are representative men, standing in for political and historical forces. But they emerge as intimately human in their wants and expectations, their hopes and undefined passions. They experience moral quandaries that are recognizable, and their relationships involve tensions, conflicts, and intimacies that are also immediately recognizable. In this sense, McMurtry, even early in his career, began to blend the realistic and romantic in a mode uniquely his own.

From the opening frame on, central preoccupations are transience and the irrevocable passage of time. This interest is most vividly captured through the first-person point of view in Lonnie himself. Recalling the past from an indeterminate present, he renders events not only as pure memories but as recollections colored by a nostalgia intensified as he remembers his own youthful perceptions, his inarticulate physical desires and resplendent hopes. As the events of the novel unfold, he is a teenager, bound to the land by a loyalty to his grandfather, provincial in his understanding of the world, but drawn by a wider world of which he has no concrete conception. This lack of experience serves only to enrich his capacity to imagine, and the loneliness of his life on the land provides among other things the freedom to ponder, to envision a future almost fantastic in its proportions. He has taken a few trips to Fort Worth, and he remembers his response to them: "Except for trips to the county-line beer joints, those few nights in Fort Worth were all I had. I guess they just amounted to a few evening walks downtown, when the city lights were flashing. But they had seemed like something rich to me" (95).

After a time, Lonnie recognizes that nothing extraordinary happened on these brief forays into the city, but he is acutely aware of his own capacity to perceive a certain magic in distant places, which is reflected both in his fascination with the city as a youth and in his ability to imbue the past with a transcendent chord of memory. This again is an echo of other works in the American tradition, in this case F. Scott Fitzgerald's *The Great Gatsby*. Lonnie's Fort Worth is Gatsby's green light as it appears at the end of the novel, signifying "the orgiastic future that year by year recedes before us." This peculiarly American imagining is linked to a distinctive blend of aspirations—an attraction to the city, to wealth, to change, to future promise, and, ironically, to a crass materialism that finds its full expression in Hud, who is himself the reality behind an otherwise otherworldly vision. Lonnie's situation, however, involves a perpetual cycle of departure and return; presumably he has left the ranch but returns to it in recollection. In telling the story of his grandfather and Hud, he endows the home he came from with the same "richness" and complexity he sensed in Fort Worth. In the intense subjectivity of Lonnie's memory and in the language through which he envisions the past, the open land and the plains of North Texas possess the same quality of embodied and heartfelt experience as the city. Distance is the imagination's source-ground in its elusive quest for identity and meaning, and it is a distance as temporal as it is geographical. The same imaginative sensibility that invested Fort Worth with romantic hope appears to him in a dream: "I dozed off about that time, and I dreamed that Granddad and I were out together, riding in the early morning. . . . The green waving acres of mesquite spread out and away from us to the south and east. I saw the highways cutting through the bright unshaded towns, and I kept expecting Granddad to say something to me. But he was relaxed, looking across the land. Finally he swung his feet into the stirrups and we rode down together into the valley toward some ranch I couldn't see, the Llano Estacado nor the old Matador" (70). Now the past is what captivates, not the lights of the cities in twilight or the streets with saloons and picture shows but the open land with mesquite and horse trails, a land more real in story than in actuality. His dream reveals the fabled West that is more an embodiment of mind than a physical place, with cattle drives, free ranges, large ranches, and intimacy between the land and its people. Lonnie's conception is rich and romantic, as well as false and far too simple. Corruption has always been there, even in the destructive practices of the ranchers themselves, but it is this vision that colors Lonnie's memory of the conflict between Homer and Hud.

From the onset and throughout the novel, Homer and Hud are marked out in starkly dichotomous terms, and the reader's sympathies are with Homer, who is benevolent and protective of his grandson, kind to his wife, loyal to his workers, and truthful in all his business dealings, even when it costs him. By contrast, Hud is angry, self-focused, deceptive, driven by a desire for wealth, and covetous of Homer's land. While Homer carefully seeks to discover the disease that infects his cattle and cooperates with the veterinarians and inspectors, Hud seeks to hide the potential threat and sell the herd. Any attempt to understand Hud's perspective is rendered impossible after he sexually assaults and finally rapes Halmea, which makes him firmly irredeemable in any kind of human terms. But a close look at the manner in which Homer's character is orchestrated must inevitably reveal him as complicated. He is the overtly mythic hero of the frontier romance transported over time to the American West. He has built a ranch out of the open range, and he is intimately bound to the land itself by forces that defy comprehension. He is governed by a reactionary principle: any change to a traditional life on the range represents corruption and degradation. In his heartfelt love for Lonnie and others, he transcends type, but, read with the actual history of North Texas in mind, he represents the very figure who displaced the (albeit brutal) Comanche, changed the grasslands into cattle range, slaughtered the American bison, and worked in tandem with the destructive farming practices that led to the Dust Bowl. His wistful reflections on the tragedy of a passing era must be understood in this context, and any sympathy he inspires must come from a deeper grasp of his tragic dilemma: he is a human being possessed of a basic integrity and commitment to people and principle, but he is caught in the sweep of a history he cannot control or understand, redeemed not by his status as mythic frontier hero bound to the land but by the basic integrity he displays, which causes him to rise above character type. This becomes clear as he considers the possibility of oil drilling on his land: "What good's oil to me. . . . What can I do with it? With a bunch of fuckin' oil wells. . . . I can't feel a smidgen a pride in 'em . . . cause they ain't none of my doin. . . . Money, yes. Piss on that kinda money. . . . I want mine to come from something that keeps a man doing for himself" (106).

This reflection displays the central values of the frontier hero and the Western mythic ideal: hard work, independence, utilitarian industry, and integrity. But, taken in the context of the era reflected clearly in his conflict with Hud, Homer's values represent a grounded ethical response to the rise and increased dominance of commercial capital and the money economy. He rejects the wealth offered by oil because it requires nothing of him in terms of labor and devotion, and by implication he stands against any business arrangement in which wealth is achieved by luck and circumstance, such as money acquired through the stock and commodities markets that so dominate the twentieth-century business climate and undergird so many modern fortunes. In this sense, he is a truly tragic figure, culpable in ways he does not grasp fully, caught by deterministic forces that in spite of their power do not entirely relieve him of responsibility. In spite of his iconic value, he is portrayed in richly human terms, and his plight is recognizable to anyone born into a set of social and historically grounded circumstances they come to depend upon and live by, circumstances that shape their very identity. Homer's values, though mythic in origin, are a measured and pointed response to a market economy gone awry. Rendered in the simple language of a North Texas rancher, they nevertheless reflect the basic outlines of any thoughtful critique of twentieth-century high capitalism.

This conflict crystallizes in the character of Hud, who embodies the avarice and malevolence that from McMurtry's point of view seem inherent in the new economy. McMurtry is not subtle in linking Hud's personal behavior to a set of values that characterize the worst impulses of an unregulated high capitalism. His vitriol and anger are present from the beginning of the novel, in his interactions with Lonnie and his disrespect for Homer and even his mother. But his selfish ambition becomes most clear when he tells Homer in no uncertain terms that he will eventually take over the ranch and use it as he sees fit. His eventual rape of Halmea should not immediately be read at a metaphorical level. He does it, Lonnie observes it, and its effects on Halmea are real and tragically consequential. But the act also becomes an elaborate metaphor quietly interpreted by Lonnie himself. Feeling quite guilty, Lonnie recalls his own sexual fantasies:

"I didn't want to do it mean, like Hud did everything, but I wanted to do it to her. I was shaking, lying there in bed. And Hud would always do the thing he wanted to do, whether it hurt anybody or not; Hud just did what he intended to do" (117). Both men are motivated by desire and want, in this case for a woman and, at a figurative level, for wealth and all it provides. But Hud's actions are bereft of ethics, rapacious both literally and metaphorically, and Lonnie's reflection lifted from the context of the plot could be used to describe many of the nameless individuals exploiting the region through banking and commodities and financial markets, as well as through the oil industry. Hud's murder of Homer, dubiously masked in his attempt to end Homer's suffering, serves only to amplify the analogy. The old way must give way to the new, and no action is too callous in orchestrating the tragic inevitability of sweeping historical and economic change. All of this is most tragically figured in the slaughter of the diseased cattle, an act in which Homer chooses to participate no matter how heart-rending the experience. As the cattle die in a mass grave, he must kill two of his favorites at point-blank range, a scene that foregrounds his own death and seems a kind of metaphorical suicide. It might be easy to read *Horseman, Pass By* as McMurtry's swan song to the Old West, but in reality, for all the novel's descriptive beauty and nostalgia, it is more aptly characterized as a lamentation, a wailing pronouncement against the exile initiated by the indifferent forces of modernity.

Leaving Cheyenne (1962)

Leaving Cheyenne, McMurtry's second novel, is set nearby in the fictional Thalia, a town based on Archer City that figures significantly in much of McMurtry's work. *Leaving Cheyenne* is imbued with the same wistful tone of nostalgia as *Horseman, Pass By.* The descriptions, language, and particularly the characters are a part of an embodied present but are linked to region in such a way as to evoke in each case a deep sense of loss. As in *Horseman, Pass By,* the ennui and rootlessness of the three major characters suggest that the past, which has faded into history, was substantial and valuable, both for the individuals who sustained and created it and for the nation that would transform it into myth. The range, the sweep of open land, the possibility offered to those who desire wealth and success and those who seek nothing but freedom remain an evocative and sympathetic reality that forms the palette of a highly personal story of relationships, emotional conflict, and love, however idiosyncratically defined. But what begins to emerge more clearly in *Leaving Cheyenne* is a theme so often missed in McMurtry's novels, whether taken individually or collectively: a deep and pointed ambivalence about the reality of Western history and the mythology that emerged from it. It is a history that differs significantly from its frequent representation in popular literature. The West was never open, given that it was always peopled. But neither was it entirely free, insofar as monied interests quickly arrived to exploit the region even before the common people, who by all accounts responded to its promise. That largely false promise was supported by the West's representation in mythological terms, in a genre that foregrounded the virtues of strength, independence, hard work, and a propensity to violence, the central figures, of course, being the gunfighter, the cowboy, and the rancher.

Leaving Cheyenne is in a broad sense a modern "Western," set in the twentieth century and revolving around the conflicts between ranchers and oilmen, mythic types in various forms and configurations. It is less burdened, perhaps, by the formal pattern of the Western that appears in the Lonesome Dove series, and as such McMurtry's careful scrutiny of the mythic hero's values is easier to see. Though he has not commented in detail on his own works, in interviews he has made it quite clear that his "Westerns" are intended not as simplistic celebrations of place and time but as critical inquiries into a complicated and morally vexing history. Any reading of character in McMurtry's Westerns should be attentive to the detailed nuances of character that are the locus of this scrutiny. Characters may resemble their mythic counterparts in other novels in the genre, and they do in fact follow the contours of the pattern. But readers must be careful not to allow their sympathies and automatic responses to the myth to overshadow the fact that these characters, as McMurtry represents them, are deeply flawed, often prone to violence, self-indulgence, indolence, and disregard for the land and people they are meant to represent and protect. They are by no means villains, but in McMurtry's hands they also transcend type. In Leaving Cheyenne, this scrutiny and purpose become even clearer than in the previous novel. Like Horseman, Pass By, the novel did not receive a significant number of reviews, but those that appeared were generally positive. In the New York Times Book Review, Marshall Sprague observed that "The people in Mr. McMurtry's Texas triptych are acutely intelligent. The book's comedy is rare, the tragedy heart-rending—and, over all, there is an atmosphere of serenity and wisdom. Gid, Johnny, and Molly were unconventional, but they knew about life and love and seized both without hesitation or regrets." He also whimsically wrote that "if Chaucer were a Texan writing today, and only 27 years old, this is how he would have written and this is how he would have felt."[2] Sprague captured the centrality of character in the novel, as well as its humor, nostalgia, and sense of place. It is in fact these elements that function interdependently to create a novel that is very much about mood and tone—in the reader's experience and in the minds of the three main characters. The narrative moves forward through a series of vacillating situations that condition the attitudes and mental states of each person involved. A whimsical ennui is the prevailing mood, as the characters respond to a peculiar and shifting set of life circumstances that they seem not to be in a position to choose or orchestrate with any kind of genuine agency.

Like so many novels set in the West, this second work takes its name from an American folksong of mysterious origin, having perhaps been written in the late nineteenth century and celebrating the trail drive. The first stanza begins, "Goodbye, old Paint / I'm a leaving Cheyenne," and this refrain is repeated in a song about a cowboy who leaves Wyoming for Montana, evoking the wistful theme of adventure and displacement that is so much a part of a substrand of American folk tunes that deal with the experiences of the Western cowboy. The novel recounts the story of three characters over a period of forty or more years: Gideon Fry, a landowning rancher; Johnny McCloud, Gid's friend in youth and his employee as they age; and, Molly Taylor, the independent, poor, yet resilient woman they both love. As the story begins, Gid and Johnny are young, and both playfully but seriously pursue Molly. Gid inherits a ranch and all the ambition and responsibility that come with it. He wants to make Molly his wife. No less in love with her but grounded in the moment, the landless Johnny is less conventional in his desires, and Molly cares for and becomes sexually intimate with them both, if only because they seem so different. From this initial situation evolves a thirty-year love triangle. For complicated reasons, Molly can commit herself fully neither to Gid nor to Johnny and instead marries a thoughtless and shallow oil worker, Eddie. Over the course of many years, she has two sons, the first by Gid and the second by Johnny. Eddie dies, both boys are killed in World War II, and the three main characters grow into old age, still committed to one another as well as to the peculiar and mysterious visions that both sustain them and keep them perpetually apart. They are witness to a changing world, but what they see is not only the land and its people in a state of transition. They are witnesses to a trauma more personal and intimate, as each of them reacts to a sense of growing impermanence by fashioning a kind of stubborn independence. They come to care for one another deeply, but transience becomes more than a social state; it takes on an existential importance, in fact the fundamental and governing reality of their lives together. In a genuine sense, they are "together" in a peculiar kind of marriage, but one that fails to fully satisfy as perhaps a more conventional relationship might. But, as the narrative proceeds, it is clear that their arrangement is the only one that makes sense given the world as they experience it.

The novel is organized into three parts, each narrated by a different character and all beginning with epigraphs from novels, folksongs, and even Chaucer. The first, "The Blood's Country," consists of twenty-four chapters and is narrated by Gid when the main characters are all young. The second, narrated by Molly in middle age, is titled "Ruin Hath Taught Me" and contains nine chapters, centered around her relationship with Gid and Johnny and the short lives of their sons. The third, "Go Turn My Horses Free," is predictably narrated by Johnny and deals with their later years as they enter their sixties. Though the novel is fairly brief given the time frame represented, it is epic in scope and imbued with a tonality of quiet grandeur typical of longer novels. Like those of *Horseman, Pass By,* its tone and mood are quite distinctive in a narrative of its length. But it is in many ways the setting, the way the landscape is described, and the characters' relationship to the land and to history that lend a kind of scope to the novel. Place, together with time and the rising tide of modernity, makes the novel emblematic and in that sense epic.

In certain ways, Gid and Johnny are prototypes for Woodrow Call and Augustus McCrae from the *Lonesome Dove* series. They are two friends, drawn together by a mutual attachment to a kind of freedom, each committed to the other but different in their fundamental approaches to life. Gid is similar to Call in his commitment to work and to accomplishment and accumulation. Johnny is a corollary to Gus in his love of freedom and enjoyment. Though drawn by McMurtry in vivid and human-like terms, both conform to the basic contours of the frontier hero in their commitment and orientation to the West itself. Yet, consistent with McMurtry's desire to revise and scrutinize the Western, they emerge as problematic heroes, at times confused and never in control of the circumstances that circumscribe them. The characters in *Leaving Cheyenne* stand on their own as developed characters, but the four figures together involve a pairing of the future-minded man of work and the present-centered man of freedom, suggesting that the Western experience in the nineteenth and twentieth centuries confronted people with similar conditions, opportunities, choices, and limitations. Only vaguely foreshadowing the *Lonesome Dove* series, *Leaving Cheyenne* more forcefully confronts the emerging conflict between the Western pastoral in the form of ranching and the commercial and industrial reality of modernity. McMurtry celebrates the pastoral, even as he perceives its harshness and limitations in portraying its passing. This can be seen in Molly's attitude toward perhaps the most common image of modernity, the automobile: "I hadn't got a car till 1941. Besides being expensive and dangerous, I thought they was just plain ugly. I couldn't understand why so many people took such an interest in them. Both the boys [her sons] were big car-lovers . . . they were both on the road constantly, going somewhere. I just let them go. Them driving didn't worry me like me driving. They grew up in a time when cars were the thing, and they knew enough about them to handle them okay" (194).

Molly's reflection captures in vivid terms the simple thoughts of a woman who is essentially the product of the nineteenth century, a person rooted in place, less drawn to movement, content with her small plot and the home she has known since birth. There is nothing idyllic in her sensibility. In that same home she has dealt with near starvation, want, physical and emotional abuse, the essential harshness of life in the rural West made more difficult because she has always lived near the bottom of a fairly rigid system of social stratification. Nevertheless, the world of simple houses, barns, small gardens, fields and scattered fences is the world she knows, clings to, and in her choices implicitly affirms. In this sense, Molly has an emblematic quality, connoting the basic human difficulty in responding even to positive historical change. Much of what constitutes progress would bring ease to her life, and the technological advances that she holds at bay would help to provide some of the freedom she quite naturally desires. But McMurtry manages to capture the fundamental human resistance to change, a resistance that posed a tremendous challenge to whole generations of people caught in the sweep of transition from the nineteenth to the twentieth century, from an older era to the new.

This transition from the pastoral to the modern is captured most fully in the contrast between and the commonality among Gid, Johnny, and Molly. As the novel begins, Gid and Johnny are both Texas boys, soon to be men. They are committed friends, familiar with work, obsessed with sex, competitive in their desire for Molly. They travel together, drink together, dream together, and in Gid's reminiscence contend in their own way for Molly's malleable affections. For all their similarity, though, Gid clearly anticipates the modern, though in a manner quite different from Hud, whose ambitions are linked to oil. Gid will inherit a ranch from his father, who has raised him to an ethic of hard work and commitment to the land he owns. In his character, McMurtry draws on actual history to evoke type. Like many figures in Westerns (and not unlike Homer Barron), Gid is a rancher, but as such he is an allegory of the modern industrialist. He dedicates himself to the land in the belief that his moral obligation, his life's purpose, is to build something tangible and material, his own realm of security and identity. He loves Molly with a genuine and deep sentiment. He is not drawn to her for any social position she can offer. But he wants to marry her and to commit her to the same vision. He reflects on these values when he is away on a venture with Johnny: "The homesickness was the worst part of it, though. I didn't mind the work, and I didn't mind the company; I didn't mind the country, or even the cold weather. I just minded feeling like I wasn't where I belonged. Home was where I belonged, but tell that to Johnny and he would have laughed like hell. He didn't feel like he belonged to any certain place, and I did" (105).

McMurtry is careful not to contrast the young men too starkly. They are from the same place and do the same work, and in many ways they share the same values. But Gid is bound to the land he knows, even as he is aware of its limitations and its less-than-redeemable qualities. He reflects clearly on the differences between his friend and himself: "When you came right down to it, Dad was right: me and him was a lot different. . . . The country might not be very nice and the people might be ornery; but it was my country and my people, and no other country was; no other people, either. You do better staying with what's your own, even if it's hard. Johnny carried his with him; I didn't. If you don't stick with a place, you don't have it very long" (105). Gid is no reactionary. His sense of home is central to his commitment to work and to progress. Considered historically, as a rancher he is an intermediary figure between past and present, since it is the oil industrialist who embodies the full force of modernity with all its commercial excess and environmental waste. But Johnny stands against all material ambition, living only for the present and seeking freedom not only from place but from the burden of ownership. It is interesting that McMurtry in essence splits the Western myth in two, presenting half of it in Gid and the other half in Johnny, and Johnny is particularly interesting in that his character involves all of the ironies built into the frontier hero myth since its inception in the American novels of the early nineteenth century. On the one hand, Johnny avoids conventional ties and limitations, maintaining his freedom at all costs. But he is a rancher and a cowboy working for Gid, and as such he serves the very interests that will transform the land, settle it, and in the end make the cowboy's life a thing of the past. It is a transition of which neither man is aware. They simply pursue their inner desires and motives. They cannot know that the range will give way to the oilfield and the town will fade in a process of urbanization. But both characters act to bring about this process, and their lack of genuine volition is clearly a part of the irony. The characters Gid and Johnny, then, are configured in a manner similar to many in the history of the genre of the American historical romance.

This can be further seen early in their relationship when Gid buys Johnny an expensive saddle. It is thing Johnny appreciates and treasures, but it remains the only "thing" he truly values. Although throughout his life he repeatedly returns home, his separation is affected not because he leaves permanently but because his approach to home is always playful and tentative. He is content to work for Gid and, in a peculiar, Thoreauvian move, to avoid the responsibility of material ambition. It is in this spirit that he approaches his relationship with Molly. Although he is no less in love with her than is Gid, their relationship is always bound to the present moment: conversation, physical joy, the mere presence of the other. In that sense, Johnny is bound only by a premodern conception of the past but one that is as mythical as any other. He is a "cowboy" clinging to a freedom that is won only at the cost of true commitment, a rare figure indeed historically, one that existed for only a short period of time but that represented a perpetual challenge to the darker consequences of ambition.

It is easy to categorize Gid and Johnny as historical types, to see their attitudes in terms of the historical forces that present them with choices. Although *Leaving Cheyenne* evokes the tensions between progress and reaction that suggest the historical romance, the interaction of character and the nuances of personality that emerge are typical of the comedy of manners. The men are products of their time and as characters are influenced by type, but in McMurtry's rendering they do not seem artificial and predictable. The fact that each has the opportunity to tell the story lends depth to their reflections, and the beautiful alchemy that emerges involves a simultaneous celebration and criticism of myth. As alternative versions of the Western hero, they point to the veracity of the myth and, at the same time, to its limitations when type conquers the human. In their deep sympathy, especially as Gid fails to consummate fully his love for Molly in marriage, we see how mythic types rendered with complete attention to the human reality demonstrate the unbreakable linkage between people and historical circumstances. This is certainly true in the character of Molly. She is strong, self-sufficient, loving, and deeply sympathetic, but her choices are vexing. Why doesn't she simply make a decision? Gid offers her stability and home, and she cares for him as he does her. The answer lies partially in her past, in the fact that she was neglected and abused, and she displays a psychology typical of that experience: "Dad always expected his kids to mind him without asking no questions. . . . But I still thought that he was an awful good daddy, and that's what Johnny and Gid could never understand. They never liked dad; neither did Eddie. But all they seen was his rough side. . . . It used to make me blue that I was the only one he had to love him. Mama and him wasn't suited for one another; Dad was rougher on her than he was on any of us" (191). This passage makes it appear that her father was a typical rural man of work: stoic, unexpressive, hard out of necessity. But this is Molly's interpretation of him after she has reflected on a circumstance in which he made her disrobe and reveal herself to her brother in the most private way. Her father tried to make her touch her brother to give him an erection, ostensibly to teach him the facts of life. But it is clear that she and perhaps the other children experienced physical and sexual abuse.

Molly's justification involves the conflicted and tortured psychology of the abused, a set of emotional reactions emerging from a desire for an appropriate parental love that has been denied her. She chooses to marry Eddie, a man not unlike her father, and refuses Gid, a man who might offer her a better life, thus demonstrating perhaps the irreparable psychology that is the consequence of abuse. This careful rendering of motivation challenges more romantic readings of her character, which might tend to celebrate her independence, particularly in her relationships with Gid and Johnny. Molly as an individual could exist anywhere, as she demonstrates a common response to her experience, but her location in the West is not inconsequential. She is born of the harshness of the land, shaped by an environment of competition and scarcity. Her choice to marry Eddie is partially explained by the fact that, unlike Gid, she is poor, and Eddie comes from the same social position. She is clearly uncomfortable with the life Gid offers her because it involves a social world she does not understand. It is with this particular attention to the psychological nuances of social stratification that McMurtry pursues her character. The social classes in the region in which Gid, Johnny, and Molly live are malleable and tend to intermingle, but they nevertheless exist. There are landowners, merchants, businessmen, and bankers, and there are those who work for them at various levels and with different levels of education. In contrast to the conventional wisdom, Molly, though clearly wounded by the past, is genuinely comfortable only with those who share her social status, and, though she loves Gid in her own way, she can never be fully comfortable with him.

In this sense, *Leaving Cheyenne* confronts many of the human issues often dealt with in the novel of manners, people in dense social contexts being shaped internally by a complex human world, but in Molly's internal conflicts McMurtry displays modern insights into the psychological consequences of social stratification. At the same time, like many of his works, this second novel in simple and poignant terms portrays the sweeping historical reality of the American West in the twentieth century, a West born of the frontier, transformed by settlement, conditioned by human seeking and the power of the imagination, and ultimately changed by the unalterable forces of modernity. All of these historical themes are rooted in people, growing up, living, working, loving, hoping, and finally growing old. After Gid's death, in his sixties, as Molly and Johnny ponder whether they should marry in old age, they conclude that the die has been cast, that they will remain as they have been. They have experienced irreparable losses—their son, their friend, their vague and indefinable hopes—but in all of this there is a sense that regret is a thing that neither can comprehend. They have lived the lives that history, nature, and circumstances have offered them, and their only choice is to continue, perceive, endure, and, most of all, remember.

CHAPTER 3

The Thalia Novels

Beginning with *The Last Picture Show,* in 1966, Thalia became iconic, the place through which McMurtry would explore his love of home as well as his deep ambivalence about its history. It might be argued that if there were ever a country within a country, Texas might be that place, and certainly McMurtry's region can claim a past like no other. But it is one that demonstrates in vivid terms the Western world's transition to late modernity. In 1889 McMurtry's grandparents moved from Missouri and purchased a piece of ranch land with good water, where they raised a large family. From that unique vantage point, they sought to make a life and witnessed North Texas in the early stages of its transformation into the twentieth century. They probably saw the last cattle drives and in some way felt the changes taking place on the land, in the hearts and minds of those who drew a living from sweeping plains under expansive skies. One can imagine that stories dealing with this experience and its emotional effects were a part of the oral history of the family, and like any oral history these stories were enriched, embellished, and changed into something that far transcended the limitations of historical chronicle. This would have been a history full of romance and faith, drawn from an intoxicating and hypnotic reverie inspired by the open land and fueled by the expansionist dreams that had captivated the nation. McMurtry was a writer from the beginning, even before he knew it, and, not unlike Lonnie Bannon, he would climb the barn at night at look out across the prairie, hearing the trucks and trains and catching with his eye the shadows of their passing as they transported goods and people west to cities on the West Coast and east to Dallas and Fort Worth. This must have been a deeply emotional experience that his young mind could not completely grasp, and he has spent much of his writing life attempting to comprehend its significance. The land itself, the tracks first laid in the nineteenth century, the modern highways, the vast twilight of a storied land already replete with hope and tragedy—all these things spoke to a sensibility that even then must have vaguely understood the universality of the experience: home, stability, place, yet transience and the inexorable passage of time, both for people and for the places they call home. It is these themes that inform what might be called the Thalia saga. Though *Horseman, Pass By* and *Leaving Cheyenne* are set near Thalia, other McMurtry novels take the town as the central setting, tracing the lives of characters that define the human texture of the town. The three most important of these are *The Last Picture Show* (1966), *Texasville* (1987), and *Duane's Depressed* (1999).

The Last Picture Show (1966)

This first novel in the Thalia saga brought McMurtry to a wider audience and garnered largely positive reviews. In the *New York Times,* Thomas Lask was guarded about the book's form and uncertain about the quality of its transitions, and he tended to favor McMurtry's portrayal of women. But Lask was firm in his sense that the novel captured the region effectively, writing that "A sorrier place would be hard to find. It is desiccated and shabby physically, mean and small-minded spiritually. Mr. McMurtry is expert in anatomizing its suffocating and dead end character." He finally concluded that the novel is "funny and brutal at the same time," with an "understanding compassion for its characters' actions and eccentricities."[1] In 1971 *The Last Picture Show* was adapted into a film directed by Peter Bogdanovich. It was nominated for eight Academy Awards, including Best Picture and Best Director, and won two, for Best Supporting Actress (Cloris Leachman) and Best Supporting Actor (Ben Johnson). In many ways, the success of the film tended to obscure the book. Recently, in the United Kingdom's *Independent,* David Evans pointed to the merits of the novel in contrast to the film, arguing that the book "has long been overshadowed by Peter Bogdanovich's much lauded film adaptation" but that "the movie is successful only to the extent that it captures the gentle comedy and elegiac tone of its source material." He also claimed that the novel is "a deeply affectionate book, and its likable protagonists, from the pool-hall king Sam the Lion to the teenage temptress Jacy, are deftly drawn."[2] It is certainly the combination of setting and character that gives the story a peculiar vitality, a strange blend of angst and sympathy.[3]

In many ways, *The Last Picture Show* evokes the same themes as McMurtry's first two novels, and, as Evans noted, it is elegiac in its portrayal of change, transition, and decay. The ranch culture that has sustained small towns throughout Texas has declined, giving way to the oil industry and the inexorable movement of people to the cities and suburbs. But thematically the book is somehow less sweeping than McMurtry's first two novels and more intimate in character psychology and relations. In one sense, little happens, which is precisely the point. Young people must contend with an uncertain future. Old people survive on memories and lament lost opportunities. Men and women in middle age struggle with disillusionment and declining hopes. Almost all of them take refuge in desperate, sad, and frequently confused encounters with one another, many of them sexual, as they attempt to find some semblance of stability and contentment. The central characters are Sonny Crawford and Duane Moore, two high school seniors and former football players who spend their time working and casually hanging out at the local pool hall. There is one failing movie theater, struggling to survive because of the birth of the television era. Both young men are captivated by Jacy Farrow, though she is dating Duane, and the novel involves a series of interactions as they seek her confused and unpredictable affections. Lost and lonely, Sonny begins an affair with Ruth Popper, the sad and emotionally neglected wife of the football coach. The town seems the outer projection of their interior lives. In seeking some kind of solace in one another, most of them cause more harm than good. Jacy is well positioned socially and cannot stay with the working-class Duane. Instead, she joins a group of wealthy but dissolute young people who share her social standing. Finding herself rejected, she becomes intimate with Sonny for a time after Duane joins the service, causing Sonny to abandon Ruth. There is little malice in any of them, and to call them selfish would be an inadequate rendering of their complexity. They languish in quiet desperation, each of them seeking a sense of human connection they cannot define.

The Last Picture Show consists of twenty-six chapters told from a third-person omniscient point of view, a rare aesthetic choice given the relative brevity of the book. Readers are given glimpses into the thoughts and feelings of many characters, even ostensibly minor ones, leading ultimately to the question of who the major characters are and whether anyone occupying this world can be considered minor. Novels of this length are frequently told from either the first-person or the third-person limited omniscient point of view. In his first two books McMurtry employed many genres but tended to emphasize themes of progress and reaction typical of the American historical romance, as the patterns of social life in the outgoing century gave way to new forms in the new one. *The Last Picture Show* retains these concerns, considering them essential, but it is perhaps more rooted in the particulars of place, with less focus on the breadth of the land and descriptions of landscape. The emphasis is on the interior lives of characters, with special attention given to how their various minds affect others. This places the novel firmly in the tradition of the social novel and the novel of manners, and the role the town plays in shaping their attitudes and behaviors makes this eminently clear.

The novel is precise in charting the social stratification in the town, from the affluent Farrows and their friends in nearby Wichita Falls to the self-sufficient but less moneyed pool-hall owner Sam the Lion, to the teachers and merchants, the roughnecks, and the working-class Sonny and Duane. This social texture is central to the novel's concerns, and McMurtry provides one of the most intimate portraits of American small-town life at midcentury, tracing its effects on the human beings who are captured by a deceptively complex dynamic that seems at times tremendously difficult to negotiate. Again, the social dimension is intimately drawn, from the first page of the novel: "Sometimes Sonny felt like he was the only human creature in the town. It was a bad feeling, and it usually came on him in the mornings early, when the streets were completely empty, the way they were one Saturday morning in late November. The night before Sonny had played his last game of football for Thalia High School, but it wasn't that that made him feel so strange and alone. It was just the look of the town" (1). Region remains central, but the details of place seem both the cause and the outer image of the characters' mood and sensibility. Ennui marks the prevailing tone of the novel, and this feeling is so strong that to call *The Last Picture Show* a satire is to contain the book within one genre too reductively. But as the story proceeds and as people react to one another, there is certainly a satirical element at play, and insofar as the role of satire is to criticize, the story certainly fulfills that purpose. But the broader goal seems to be to provide a vivid and detailed picture of one dimension of American life in the postwar period, as the social fabric of the nation unravels and is rewoven into a new and more complex tapestry that individuals, especially young ones, find difficult to understand.

In subsequent volumes in the Thalia saga, the protagonist is clearly Duane Moore, but in *The Last Picture Show* Sonny Crawford is significantly more prominent. If a protagonist must be defined, it is Sonny. He carries the mood of the novel most fully, its exhaustion and sadness, its sense of longing and clinging hope. Although the thoughts of many characters are rendered, Sonny's consciousness dominates, and after Duane's eventual and temporary departure, Sonny remains. The story recounts his friendship with Duane, his dispassionate relationship with another young girl, his secret longing for Jacy, his sadly destructive affair with Ruth Popper, his conversations and reflections with Sam the Lion, and his eventual brief encounter with Jacy.

In many ways, Sonny is a typical youth, and McMurtry is careful to dismantle the sacrosanct notion in American culture that high school is somehow an ideal time. Instead, for Sonny, it is a time of confusion, indecision, preoccupation with girls together with all the associated insecurities, and the peculiar dread and quiet anxiety that occur when the simplicities of childhood no longer satisfy. All the young people in the novel experience emotions related to this difficult transition, Sonny perhaps most clearly and completely. These are universal experiences with the same contours no matter the locale, but the setting of the novel certainly contributes to Sonny's concerns. His problem begins with his relationship with his girlfriend, Charlene. Sonny doesn't much care for her, nor she him, and both of them seem to be passing the time under the assumption that it is marginally better to have a high school relationship than not. Without admitting it, Sonny, together with other boys, is intensely attracted to Jacy, and though his jealousy of Duane is never mean-spirited, he nevertheless envies him. After his anticlimactic breakup with Charlene, Sonny finds himself involved with Ruth. McMurtry orchestrates the development of this relationship with tremendous care, as he describes the events, the physical details of their encounters, and the thoughts that attend them, particularly Ruth's. She has been utterly neglected by her husband, in some ways physically but primarily at an emotional level. She is middle aged, lonely, in need of intimacy, and largely bereft of hope. Their relationship begins with a kiss and moves on quickly, without the least suspicion from her clueless, insensitive, and self-absorbed husband. For Ruth, the sexual aspect of their relationship is tremendously important and satisfying, but it is deeply bound to a sense of emotional intimacy and closeness, an indescribable bond that for a time is a fortress against her lost hope and quiet despair. Sonny is never malevolent, and at some level he understands her emotional plight, but when the opportunity with Jacy presents itself late in the novel he abandons Ruth, his own confusion and bumbling attempts to find meaning conflicting with his obligation to the older woman. Their relationship is the most developed example of the dynamic that typifies each interaction, as characters connect only to destructively disconnect, damaging and harming one another in a hopeless quest to satisfy indefinable desires that have a physical dimension but are also deeply psychological. This pattern is central to the social novel, as the interiors of character are altered and influenced by the exterior world and the people who give it human contours, textures, and characteristic features.

Another distinctive, clumsy, and in this case only mildly destructive relationship involves Jacy Farrow and Duane Moore. On the surface, it is a typical high school relationship, with its dates, silly intrigues, meaningless conflicts, and physical interaction that ultimately concludes in an awkward sexual encounter one might expect of people their age. On the one hand, McMurtry creates a whimsical sense of romance and nostalgia, and the characters' interactions are recognizable, endearing, and at times quite funny. But, in the spirit of the social novel, there are deeper issues at work. Jacy is extremely attractive, and many boys desire her. Duane's attraction to her is motivated by her beauty but also by her social stature. Her father has made a fortune in oil, and his family is positioned at the top of the social ladder; this is partly why Duane and Sonny find her appealing. Her attraction to Duane is volatile, tentative, and consti- tuted in different terms. Jacy experiences a confused sexual awakening bound up with a peculiar and awkward search for self. Complicating this transition is her mother, who is a former beauty, disillusioned with her married life and the opportunities the town has offered her. She opposes the idea of Jacy having a long-term relationship with Duane, but she has no problem with Jacy sleeping with him. Her ideas are motivated not by any sense of sexual liberation but by an emotional exhaustion that renders moral considerations largely irrelevant. Practically, her mother knows Jacy should marry a man who will make her comfortable, but this will not result in any deep satisfaction. We learn of her mother's past, only to find that her only meaningful relationship came early in her marriage through an affair with Sam the Lion, the admirable and sympa- thetic owner of the pool hall, who acts as a father figure to Duane, Sonny, and a mentally handicapped boy, Billy. The advice Jacy receives from her mother fur- ther confuses and confounds her, and Jacy unintentionally toys with Duane's emotions, is used by a group of socialites, and, in an attempt to get her parents' attention, briefly elopes with Sonny. Her bumbling attempts to seek her own purpose, to distinguish genuine value from the beauty of her youth, and her desire to find a coherent self lead her to hurt Duane and Sonny quite deeply. If not exactly selfish, she is without question self-focused, and, like the actions of many of the characters in the novel, her seeking has human consequences in the pain she causes the young men she encounters. Certainly, Sonny and Duane are more resilient than Ruth Popper and the destruction to their feelings repair- able, but the dynamic is the same. Characters in a state of confusion and doubt attempt to find themselves in another person, only to harm the person instead.

Thus, the novel, though full of humor and good will, is a detailed explora- tion of human interiors and exteriors, of minds that seek and relationships that stumble and fail. It is fundamentally a psychological novel in the tradition of the novel of manners, imbued with a prevailing sense of ennui. Historical con- text aside, *The Last Picture Show* concerns itself with the human capacity to dream of the future and the world's capacity to erode rather than shatter those dreams. But it is also a story that speaks playfully to an imperfect humanity, pointing to the less-than-devastating tendencies to hurt others in a desperate search for meaning. It is this search, though, that in subtle yet obvious ways redeems the characters. Their capacity for hope, their ability to transform the mundane reality of the daily lives into a vivid landscape of hope and desire—these things speak to their recognizable humanity. Taken in context, their plight is distinctly postwar, as the transformation from the rural to the modern functions to displace them from the life they have been taught to expect. The image of the failing movie theater will take on a portentous meaning in *Texasville,* and here it foreshadows not so much decay but transformation, as the town of Thalia and its people seek to find themselves amid the expansion of the cities and the rise of the oil industry. *The Last Picture Show* is in this sense an elegy for a place not so much gone as lost to itself and its people, and the story in its own way ends tentatively, the novel itself being only the first in a saga that continues to explore the evolving lives of a group of complex individuals. This portrayal is perhaps McMurtry's most notable accomplishment. Lack of education and a rural setting do nothing to simplify people and place but enrich them, imbuing them with color and contrast and never subjugating their sympathy to their flaws and failures.

Texasville (1987)

This second novel in the Thalia saga shifts its primary focus, with Sonny still an important character but Duane the protagonist. Duane has entered the oil business and achieved great success. But it is the 1980s; he is now middle aged, and the boom has turned to bust. The town of Thalia is preparing for its centennial celebration in which it re-creates the historical town of Texasville. Even though Duane, along with virtually everyone in the town, is facing bankruptcy, the townspeople all see Duane as a kind of intellectual and moral leader, and the novel deals with his quandaries, his traumas with family, and his many dubious relationships, all in a seemingly lighthearted but in the end starkly satirical manner. The novel explores the effects of rampant consumerism and the contours and textures of rural Texas, and the story is a playful but biting inquiry into the nature of American small-town life, which, though often portrayed as simple and virtuous, appears in *Texasville* as deeply flawed, with its pervasive alcoholism, drugs, infidelity, angst, quiet loneliness, and ennui.[4] The novel received generally positive reviews, many critics pointing to its value as entertainment but recognizing the parody and the satirical center of the book. In the *New York Times,* Michiko Kakutani wrote: "The novel shifts, page by page, from low slapstick into melancholia and back into black-humored farce; it becomes apparent that Mr. McMurtry has found an elastic narrative voice that fluently accommodates such shifts and also carries the reader with ease through some of the story's hokier scenes. . . . All in all, it makes for a wonderfully digestible book that leaves a lingering cloud of sadness in the reader's mind."[5]

Taking exception to the structure but understanding the book as a novel of manners with its focus on character interrelations, Jonathan Yardley in the *Washington Post* claimed that "*Texasville* is a big ol' mess of a book: long, haphazardly plotted" but also asserted that "the novel's intelligence and compassion are what really matter, and in this, *Texasville* is of a piece with all of McMurtry's best work."[6] Noting again the emphasis on the appealing yet deplorable flaws of the people in Thalia, as well as the skill with which McMurtry deals with setting and scene, in the *New York Times Book Review* Louise Erdrich referred to the novel's "unrestrained humor" and its "raw, material decadence" and claimed that "the individual scenes are sharp, spare, full of longhorn humor and color."[7] Critics observed and admired the skill with which McMurtry was able to mix a scathing social critique with a genuine sympathy and love for his characters.

Humor abounds even as the novel introduces Duane, who is frustrated at the circumstances of a life that has ceased to make sense. This is reflected in the fact that he avoids sex with his wife, Karla, whom, ironically, he loves. He routinely goes to the Dairy Queen to meet acquaintances and frequently has affairs with various women in the town, many of them married to people he knows well. Karla does the same, and they are quite open about it, though neither is satisfied with the arrangement. Their children are largely irresponsible. Their daughter Nellie playfully jumps from marriage to marriage, occasionally having children along the way. Their son Dickie, emerging into adulthood, is selling and using drugs while moving from woman to woman without concern, and much to Duane's dismay he and Dickie occasionally share a sexual partner. Amid all of this, they prepare for the town's centennial celebration, which is the culminating event of the novel and is portrayed as emblematic of the disorder, absurdity, and peculiar sadness of their collective lives. While all this is going on, Duane's high school girlfriend and first love, Jacy, returns from Italy and settles again in Thalia. She has orchestrated a minor career as an actress in Italian B movies, has been married and divorced, and has had children. When she returns, she quickly becomes friends with Karla and joins and marginally controls the Moore household, heightening the disorder and comedy of an already comic situation. The novel is a long and loosely structured series of episodes told in the third-person omniscient, organized in ninety-eight chapters around the preparation for the centennial and the anticipation of bankruptcy. What emerges in this lengthy narrative is a work of remarkable human sympathy, as characters who invite criticism also evoke a deep sense of identification.

The element of satire characteristic of the novel of manners emerges at the beginning of *Texasville* and is consistently maintained throughout the narrative. The story centers on a constant and compelling series of interactions and interrelationships that are interlaced with Duane's reactions and interior reflections. There is an intense though playful psychological dimension to the novel, which appears in Duane's thoughts and speech and is revealed in other characters through dialogue and action. Duane's employee and friend, Bobby Lee (who appears also in *Duane's Depressed*), spends much of his time drunk, pondering various conspiracies and anxiety-provoking possibilities, such as terrorist attacks directed, strangely, at Thalia. The town banker Lester Marlow's anxiety and depression appear with regularity, and Karla's frustration with the inadequacies of her marriage are at the heart of every conversation she has with Duane, though in each case their attachment becomes increasingly clear. McMurtry renders the town and its people as inconsequential and absurd. The fact that Thalia typifies the American small town becomes essential to the novel's themes and in the end suggests that the "town" as a social unit is an important thread in the fabric of American life. But it is an America that must elicit laughter as well as tears, as is revealed in the opening paragraph: "Duane was in the hot tub, shooting at his new doghouse with a .44 Magnum. The two-story doghouse was supposedly a replica of a frontier fort. He and Karla had bought it at a home show in Fort Worth on a day when they were bored. It would have housed several Great Danes comfortably, but so far had housed nothing. Shorty, the only dog Duane could put up with, never went near it" (9).

This opening image captures the essence of the novel's mood and the angst of its many characters, while at the same time pointing to the sources of their frustration and emptiness: commercialism and the unconscious avoidance of an interior life. *Duane's Depressed* foregrounds the human need for a meaning that can be achieved only through self-discovery and the life of the mind, and *Texasville* charts the consequences of failing to recognize this essential truth. Life has taken hold of Duane Moore, and he has always been a simple working part in the mechanics of history. He has been the beneficiary of circumstance, and now he faces becoming its victim. Together with Duane and Karla, many in the town have responded to their unexpected fortunes with material excess, but it is clear that their forays into rampant consumerism are an expression of a deeper need for meaning and purpose. The two-story doghouse that goes unused by the small dog Shorty is a humorous and evocative image connoting the ill use to which the many characters have dedicated their wealth. Duane's frustrated response reveals both his growing recognition of his error and his inability to change, as he responds to excess with the same excess, taking the object slowly apart with perhaps the most powerful handgun in existence, a firearm for which he can have no use.

The idea that the doghouse is a "replica of a frontier fort" creates a poignant and satirical contrast to the past, as the Texas of the heroic frontier is reduced to a naked man in a hot tub shooting at a silly reproduction that has served no purpose. This sense of confusion is reflected in Karla's notion that "you could make anything happen if you spent enough money" (9). She has always known at some level that her approach was flawed, but money is what they have and all they have to spend. Throughout the novel they search for more interior resources, perhaps without knowing it, as the world falls apart around them. This becomes clear as McMurtry clarifies Duane's history: "He had started poor, become rich, and now was losing money so rapidly that he had come to doubt that much of anything was true, in any sense. He had eight hundred and fifty dollars in the bank and debts of roughly twelve million, a situation that was becoming increasingly untenable" (11).

Duane's circumstances provide a vivid picture of the peculiarities and strange injustices of modern commercial capitalism. One becomes rich because of circumstances that are largely beyond one's control or understanding, by the global demand for a natural resource that just happens to be there and that requires little skill but only capital and effort to exploit. As that global demand ebbs (in this case because of OPEC), so decline the profits. What remains are the habits of excess that continue even after the bust. Duane and Karla can continue for a time to spend as if they are rich, though they are millions in debt. The system permits it, as it will permit them to declare bankruptcy and retain at least a portion of what they have gained. Duane is acutely aware of his situation, and Karla is as well, but it is Duane's job not so much to encourage that they curb their excess but to manage the situation in such a way that they can avoid catastrophe for as long as possible. This is Thalia's dilemma as a whole, and the workers, bankers, and other oilmen look to Duane not only as perhaps the smartest among them but, ironically, as their ill-suited moral compass. The novel, then, is a critique of commercial capitalism; as such, it is a vivid psychological inquiry into the social and individual human consequences that occur when that system goes awry.

But alongside this social inquiry is a more intimate exploration of the people who live and work in a fairly typical American small town in the 1980s. The "town" is no longer the center of American life. It sustains itself on one industry, and many residents have left for the opportunities that cities offer. In *Texasville*, what remains is a lovely group of pathetic characters who struggle to survive. Of course there are Duane and Karla, with their peculiar attachment and regular infidelities. But a number of characters from *The Last Picture Show* reappear, in many cases in quite different form. Sonny is the town mayor and the owner of two local businesses, including a convenience store. But, sadly, the picture show haunts him, and he is plagued by nostalgia, perhaps brought on by the early onset of dementia. He lives alone, sees Duane occasionally, and watches entire films in his head as he falls into hypnotic states that doctors cannot diagnose. In this comic novel, he evokes the most pathos as he becomes the emblematic victim of the changes in the town, which has decayed and been revived only tentatively because of the oil boom.

In contrast, Ruth Popper, the previously sad and bereft wife of the football coach, has recovered and found her way. She now works as Duane's secretary, living, it seems, quite happily as a divorcee, and she acts as Duane's adviser and as a kind of mother figure. At one point, she offers to quit her job because she knows Duane can't afford her, and it takes some work for him to convince her to stay. Given her state in *The Last Picture Show,* she suggests in no uncertain terms the possibility of recovery from a bad marriage and even from the depths of profound depression. Even though Sonny hurt her in years past, she takes care of him when he is at his worst and with her strength and fortitude becomes his optimistic counterpoint. Lester Marlow, the once-privileged young man who was a part of the elite social group that attracted Jacy, is now the town banker, and he spends the entire novel in desperate fear of incarceration because of his unnamed but clearly dubious financial activity during the boom and the bust. There is Bobby Lee, Duane's employee, with his conspiracy theories, personal sensitivities, and bad moods; Susie Nolan, the free-spirited and sexually promiscuous wife of Duane's friend Junior, who carries on simultaneous affairs, quite free of guilt, with Duane and his son Dickie, whom she openly prefers. The town is peopled by a host of major and minor characters of this sort, all endearing, all sad and comic, all indicative of the human consequences of social change. In this sense, the novel continues with the preoccupation of most of McMurtry's previous work, as the sweeping progress of history leaves whole communities changed in its wake. The town will exist only perhaps for a time as it exploits its oil. It may even recover. But, in the face of modernity, its people will remain perpetual outsiders in a world of corporations, cities, suburbs, and an unpredictable world economy. All these forces form the stage upon which the people of Thalia must act without any real understanding of what they face.

This tragicomic circumstance with all its emblematic implications for the nation as a whole works even more thoroughly at an individual level. McMurtry's genuine aesthetic sleight of hand in *Texasville* is to integrate fully the social and the individual, the historical and the psychological. Thalia is presented as typical of the American small town, much like others that have appeared in literature and film, but in its slow decline we come to see the "town" for what it is: a conglomeration and community of discrete individuals, who draw a kind of desperate sustenance from one another. In McMurtry's terms, they are not entirely individuals but threads in a fabric, and it is both the individual threads and the fabric itself that possess discrete identities. This is captured in an extended metaphor in which the housekeeper tears up a piece of cloth:

> The day before, Minerva had needed some rags and had torn up an old sheet to make them. . . . The sheet had been washed many times and was very thin. . . . He [Duane] and Karla had slept on it hundreds of times. And yet in five minutes it had stopped being a sheet and become rags. . . . Everything, it seemed, had been washed too many times, had worn too thin. . . . His friendships and his little romances . . . had once been the comfortable and reliable fabric that was his life. . . . At some point a toenail or an elbow had poked through, and now it was all tearing. (470–471)

McMurtry is often characterized as a writer of sparse prose with vivid plot and character-driven narratives, but frequently in the course of a novel he develops metaphors that convey his theme and draw from images integral to the setting. In a novel centered on a blend of family and community, he employs a domestic image to convey an intense and disturbing psychological insight. Duane's identity and happiness depend significantly on his capacity to think and reflect, a fact that again becomes clearer in *Duane's Depressed*. But in the metaphor of the worn sheet and in the tradition of great social novelists such as Austen, Dickens, and James, Duane's psychological stability is dependent on a fabric of relationships. It is not that these people have departed. Most of them remain, but over time Duane has come to feel their dependence in such a way that the stability he drew from them has worn thin and become unreliable. He feels alone among them, even as they seek his quiet wisdom and sustenance. Karla and Jacy, who often tease him and on the surface appear to depend more on each other than on him, draw a reserve of calm and solidity from Duane. In the course of the novel Jacy loses a child and Karla confesses that, in spite of their infidelities and her lively friendship with Jacy, she wants no husband but Duane. Ironically, there is an energy to all the characters' interactions, and members of the town take themselves quite seriously as they prepare for the centennial celebration, but with an increasingly clear insight Duane is able to see through a façade that others don't even recognize.

It is that celebration that becomes the grand symbol of the town, the people, their situation, and in many ways the situation of the nation as a whole. They are set to celebrate the history of the town and its link to the old historical town of Texasville. A committee has organized an event with plays, parades, games, commemorations, even a visit from the governor. The event is a blend of history and religion, of solemn celebration and drunken debauchery. Duane is on the event committee and will play Adam to Jacy's Eve in a silly skit that reenacts the creation of the world. There will be a parade and covered wagons recalling the past, as well as a set of speeches extolling the virtues of the town and its history. But, inevitably, circumstances conspire against them. The celebration begins with a dust storm that sends tumbleweeds the size of small houses through the town. The governor's helicopter cannot land because of the wind. The wagon train gets lost on the plain, and Duane has to recover the passengers with an oil truck. In the end, a group of children, led by Duane's twins, raid a truck and cover the town in broken eggs. Amid all of this, the newspaper tells the townspeople that the price of Middle Eastern oil has gone down, ensuring their ruin. Still the town celebrates, with a peculiar blend of seriousness and comic irreverence. The Baptist preacher who has tried to stop the drinking during the celebration is routed. The roughnecks become drunk. Bobby Lee accidently drives a truck into a historical building, and the town leaders, Duane excepted, take it all quite seriously. This grand crescendo of the tragicomic brings the novel to a close with little actual closure. *Texasville,* then, becomes more a state than a statement. The town and its people, the "town" as an idea, with its peculiar dependencies conditioned by historical circumstances, typify the nation as a whole. The town is simultaneously tentative and essential. Its future is uncertain, but its comic beauty and vulnerability still remain.

Duane's Depressed (1999)

Duane's Depressed concludes the last important episode in the saga, exploring the twilight years of Duane Moore, after his children have grown and he has stabilized his economic life. Sadly, he finds himself in a state of quiet despair that is deeper and less traceable than his unhappiness in the previous two novels. *Duane's Depressed* achieved generally positive reviews, many critics noting a thematic departure from the previous two books and characterizing it as a somewhat surprising culmination of a human story that reflects nearly an entire lifetime. Noting McMurtry's skill in shifting from historical novels to stories set in his own time, Nancy Pate in the *Orlando Sentinel* called *Duane's Depressed* "entertaining . . . The best contemporary novel McMurtry has written in years."[8] Many reviews took note of the novel's tone and dealt directly with the story's entertainment quality, but even in these general assessments there was an implicit endorsement of how McMurtry drew his characters, since he seemed always mindful of their incarnations in previous novels. Referring to the indefinable quality of feeling that seems to make the novel distinctive, Judith Wynn in *The Boston Herald* wrote that the book "abounds with wonderfully funny characters all lovingly graced with the light-hearted compassion that is McMurtry's hallmark."[9] The general assessment was that *Duane's Depressed* is an appealing and compelling novel that modulates between the ennui of the title and a sense of rediscovery and reformation, as Duane yet again struggles and now partially succeeds in reformulating his identity in the face of circumstances only partially of his own making.

It is interesting to note that McMurtry saw *Duane's Depressed* as a novel that reflected his own rebirth after quadruple-bypass surgery. Though Duane Moore is recognizably the same character as in the previous two novels, there is an unmistakable biographical element in his psychological state. After surgery, McMurtry said that "I was one person up until the morning of December 2, 1991. . . . When I woke up from the operation, after twelve hours in deep anesthesia, I began—although I didn't realize it immediately—my life as a different person—my life as someone else." *Duane's Depressed* emerged from this experience; despite its accurate title, the novel is about an aging man's slow rebirth and personal transformation rather than the depression itself. As the story begins, Duane is sixty-two years old and emotionally lost. His family, though endearing, is in varying states of dysfunction and disrepair. His daughters Nellie and Julie leave their children with Duane and Karla as they travel, living dissolute and indolent lives. His son Dickie returns from drug rehab after multiple attempts to get clean, and his other son, Jack, wanders the countryside hunting and adopting oddly survivalist practices. Duane loves them all, but they have disappointed him, and, though he cannot comprehend exactly where he erred, Duane quietly blames himself. As an oilman who has experienced rises, busts, and moderate recovery, he has built his life on materialism and acquisition, though he has always been both the victim and the beneficiary of circumstance and historical accident, never entirely acting on his own volition. Now, in response to a feeling of angst and hopelessness, he decides to change his ways. He gets rid of his truck and takes up walking and moves from his home full of children and grandchildren to a cabin outside town. For a time he retains his business, and his ninety-year-old secretary, Ruth Popper, and his longtime employee Bobby Lee try to understand what has changed him. He eventually seeks a psychiatrist, Honor Carmichael, who revives his waning sense of romance and sexuality, and she helps to orchestrate his recovery. Tragically, his friend Sonny dies of natural causes, and his wife, Karla, dies in a car accident. Duane's transformation takes an even more unexpected but subtle turn as he retires from his business and begins keeping a vegetable garden, donating his produce to passing strangers. The novel again takes character as central and is never strident in its social critique, but Duane himself quietly turns from materialism to a life of simplicity and reserve and, in doing so, finds a kind of redemption in spite of significant loss.

Although *Duane's Depressed* is primarily an interior journey into the mind of a man in distress, Duane's mild and far-from-uncommon trauma is clearly linked to the circumstances of his life, the choices he has made, and the historical forces that have motivated those choices. The pervasive sense of angst that so dominated the first two novels in the saga prevails here as well, but there is a deeper pathos that makes the book less satirical. Duane is no saint. He has ignored his marriage, had numerous affairs, spent money during the oil boom without reserve, and devoted less effort to his children's upbringing than they apparently needed. But he is no different from anyone else in Thalia, and certainly no different from his wife, Karla, who has been equally promiscuous and irresponsible. The greatest destructive force in the lives of all of them has again been wealth itself, the rampant materialism that characterized the oil boom but may be taken to characterize contemporary American consumer culture in general. This can be seen in the first chapter in the conflicting image of his carport:

> The carport was a spacious affair, built to house six cars in the days when cars still had some size; now that cars had been miniaturized—as had horses—the carport could accommodate ten vehicles . . . the spacious carport mainly housed a collection of junk: welding tools, old golf clubs, fishing equipment, baby carriages whose tires had been flat for several years, couches and chairs that had stalled, somehow, on their way to the upholsterer, and towering pyramids of objects acquired by Karla and one of the girls at garage sales, department stores, swap meets, or discount malls. (4)

As in *Texasville,* McMurtry is careful from the novel's inception to center Duane and his problems firmly in the context of a consumer culture gone wildly astray. Ultimately, Duane Moore might be seen as the outcome of the transformations lamented by Homer Bannon in *Horseman, Pass By.* But Homer's concern is more centered on the idea that, with oil, people are somehow displaced from creating the wealth that sustains them. In Duane's case, while oil does come from the ground ready to refine, its extraction has required effort, and Duane's has been a life of productivity and hard work. Instead, though, the consumer culture of Duane and Karla Moore is corrupt not so much in a wasted effort at the onset but in the profligate waste that emerges when wealth leads to consumption that exceeds the consumer's capacity to absorb and enjoy. The psychological complexity of this situation is considerable and compelling. In a garage-sale and swap-meet world, people sell objects that are still functional but that no longer satisfy, and other people buy them without needing them in the hope that they will fulfill a sense of undefinable longing, only to find that they are only objects, which in the end are useless. The image McMurtry captures, of "golf clubs," "welding tools," and endless secondhand objects, works as a grand metaphor for American consumer culture in the post–World War II period, and the victims are not only those who are left without in an economy that is callous in the distribution of wealth. Those who possess are victims as well, as their lives are consumed by their own confused desire, which they have directed, in the absence of more indefinable and altruistic human goals, toward the acquisition of things. This is the primary source of Duane Moore's "depression," and though the novel is focused mainly on Duane, that emotional state seems to affect most of the people in Thalia in one way or another.

McMurtry has proved to be one of the most successful authors in having his work adapted to the screen, and, though *Duane's Depressed* has yet to be filmed, it displays aspects of McMurtry's method that are distinctively cinematic. There are occasional passages of exposition that reveal a character's state of mind, but psychological complexities and difficulties are more commonly revealed through actions and dialogue. However, early in the novel, one passage makes apparent the extent to which individuals in the novel are bound to one another at an emotional level, no matter how much they have neglected one another. Karla and Duane have strayed sexually, have separated themselves from each other, and, like many in Thalia, have never lived a conventional marriage. But Karla is deeply attuned to Duane's state of mind, and her response to him is emotional at the deepest level. After Duane begins behaving in a peculiar way, Karla begins to worry intensely:

> Karla was so upset by the thought of Duane walking around in a norther that she felt a panic attack coming on. . . . (9)
>
> They had never in their lives been strangers to each other, she and Duane; but, once she thought about it a few more minutes, sitting in her car with the motor idling, she realized that the part about them not being strangers wasn't quite true. Living with Duane *had* become sort of like living with a stranger. . . . somehow forty years of constant intimacy had betrayed them finally, in some sly way. (12–13)

Duane abandons his pickup truck, having realized he has spent much of his life behind the wheel. He has taken up walking along the dusty roads in the heat, rain, and wind, acting with a strange obstinacy that disturbs Karla deeply. She doesn't fear that he is having an affair, since they have both had more than a few. But she does fear that he wants a divorce. In following him in a state of genuine panic, she tries to convince herself that perhaps divorce is the next rational step, but, in the remarkable psychological density of McMurtry's method, this is a matter of pure rationalization. Her panic attack ebbs as panic attacks do, but she is left with the cold realization that she exists in a state of uncertainty with respect to her marriage. She is a finely tuned barometer that measures Duane's state of mind, his depression prompting her intense anxiety, which, as he continues his peculiar behavior, ebbs and flows with a strangely predictable regularity. Her realization is only partly accurate. There is a distance between them; they have been strangers in a certain way. But their intimacy is deep in the sense that their minds function together, separate though they may be physically. True to the psychological dimensions of the social novel at its best, characters' psychology functions not in isolation but in a complex matrix of relationships that blur the boundaries between human interiors and exteriors.

Duane's "depression" is perhaps not clinical or at least not depression as commonly understood in that McMurtry chooses to make it an inherent part of Duane's personality or physiology. Throughout the three novels Duane displays a rich interiority, a thoughtful nature that is perpetually at odds with the circumstances of his daily life and the unpredicted successes and failures that have defined it. The materialism that has largely laid waste to his family life and compromised his marriage is something that has always left him vaguely unsatisfied, and that vagueness is no less real as he enters his sixties. What distinguishes him in *Duane's Depressed* is its intensity and the fact that he chooses to act as he has never done before. His actions are strangely humorous in that they are incomprehensible to those around him. As he takes to walking instead of driving and simplifies his living arrangements, he slowly disassociates himself from his business and in less than subtle ways distances himself from people and retreats into himself. His actions are easily interpreted, even readable in a sense, and the quiet comedy of the novel is that other characters are so immersed in their world that they cannot understand what is happening. Duane is reacting, as he enters his twilight years, to the seeming hopelessness of a life spent acquiring, spending, and responding to the exigencies of an unpredictable economy. His life is by no means over. Honor Carmichael even predicts that he has perhaps two decades to live, and he now decides to take action to change the direction of his life. He begins with moderate acts of simplification, but the genuine pathos of the novel comes from the fact that he acts without a full understanding of what ails him. Materialism is part of it, but one senses that his state of mind is in many ways existential and universal and that people of his reflective nature will experience such emotions regardless of the circumstances. His transition, then, is volitional rather than predictive, and he acts without even a moderate understanding of its consequences. He acts, in a sense, on instinct.

Perhaps the most striking and consequential decision he makes is to see a psychiatrist. He does so almost by accident. As he contemplates his own perceived failures with his children, he talks to Carmichael, the owner of a local convenience store. Carmichael's daughter Honor has become a successful psychiatrist in Wichita Falls, not far away. In the end Duane decides to see her. She seems to recognize quickly a significant aspect of his problem, his connection to the past and its relation to his identity. In recommending that he read Marcel Proust's *Remembrance of Things Past,* she hopes to encourage him to reflect on his own life, not in a negative sense but in order to allow him to sort out its complexities through memory. Duane is reluctant and has never been a reader, but he is motivated to read the book because he has developed a trust in her and also because she has awakened him sexually. McMurtry is quite subtle in effecting Duane's transformation, and during the process Duane must endure the loss of Karla and Sonny.

We mostly see his slow rediscovery of a new self through his actions. But there is one moment that reveals the level of Duane's emotional distress. During one of his appointments with Honor, he experiences a rush of emotion in which his lungs seem to swell; he breaks out in tears and tries to leave her office. Duane does not reveal in this scene precisely what is bothering him, but he has already revealed his concern while in an only slightly less emotional state earlier in the novel. Recalling an old man he had known who used to make fishing lures along the Red River, Duane associates him with a different and simpler time; standing alongside the river, he reflects: "Now the old man was gone and his stories too. . . . As he [Duane] watched the river the sad feeling grew sharper. . . . In coming to the edge of the old famous river—the river the cattlemen dreaded because of its quick sands, the river the Indians fought to keep and failed to keep . . . he had come suddenly to the edge of his life. He had gone as far as he could with the work he knew, with the people he knew, with the family he had helped to create. In those spheres little more could be expected" (330).

This moment of epiphany leads him into critical reflection on himself— his lack of education, his dearth of accomplishments when considered against those of more worldly people—and he desperately wants to do something more with the rest of his life. But he fears that at his age the effort would be fruitless. These concerns are bound to the river and his sense of history. Duane's is not an individualist's dilemma. It is bound to his emerging and torturous sense of what can be accomplished in the world beyond acquisition and wealth, and it is bound as well to his sense of a storied past, in which people have acted on their dreams, come to Texas from other places, and built something valuable out of the land and themselves. Subsequent generations have corrupted their efforts partly under the influence of a materialist modernity, but their lives had a meaning that seems always embedded, however suppressed, in Duane's consciousness, as a human being, a Texan, and an American. As the people in his life slowly leave him and as he leaves them to find another way, he is pressed to act in accordance with these half-understood impulses, and after his experience in therapy he becomes more active and aware as he reconstitutes his life on more simple terms.

Duane's transformation and rebirth are quiet but profound. Previously, he has been more than frustrated at the world he has allowed to circumscribe his actions, a world that leaves behind "beer cans, bottles, empty cans of motor oil . . . an old pick plastic hair dryer that someone had thrown out," and he becomes angry when he considers them next to "the white birds and green field" (158). As he comes to understand something of himself, his actions reveal that he has become more conscious of the world around him. He has begun by walking and by living in a cabin, for reasons he doesn't quite comprehend, acting more from feeling and impulse than from rationally motivated choice. But, as the novel concludes, he comes to understand that with the rest of his life, he can write a new chapter without repudiating the past. His transformation is in large part initiated by Honor, who tells him that the life he has chosen, a life of work and family, is not enough, that he is the type of person who requires more. He has always wanted to travel, and after his emotional release Honor encourages him to do so. In the end he leaves for a trip to Cairo and Rome. The heartfelt ending is quite evocative, as he writes a loving letter to Karla as if she were alive, burying it in a wooden box on her grave. This change in the saga's main character is as dramatic as any to be found in McMurtry's work, but it is the natural outgrowth of the events and circumstances the three novels have developed over the span of nearly fifty years. There is a deep sense of tragedy and inevitability: Karla, Sonny, and Jacey have died, and Duane is alone. But his children are well considering their circumstances, and Duane will take the lessons of his life into a future of promise, which he ponders in the last line of the novel, as he looks at the white boats on the Mediterranean Sea.

CHAPTER 4

The Houston Trilogy

During the late 1960s, McMurtry's work made a significant albeit temporary shift to the present. Many of his earlier novels were set in contemporary times, but, drawing from the historical romance tradition and its interest in the forces of progress and reaction, they dealt with the manner in which the past bears upon and in many ways conditions the present. In the three novels that became known as "the Houston Trilogy," McMurtry delved into the present and responds to it on its own terms. In *Moving On* (1970), *All My Friends Are Going to Be Strangers* (1972), and *Terms of Endearment* (1975), McMurtry moved away from the oil fields and ranges, from the small towns and highways, to the heart of the city and specifically to the suburb.[1] He created a complex and varied set of characters that explore perhaps the most common contemporary experience. As he understood the human complexities that emerged from the transition from ranch culture to oil culture, so he now attempted to explore the conflicts that emerged as cities expanded and suburban life became a common mode of living in America. The suburb was yet another attempt to significantly improve the daily lives of middle-class Americans, with their single-family homes, yards, and parks and their communities marked by decreased congestion and careful planning. But suburbs brought with them unintended social and psychological consequences. As people moved from tightly knit urban neighborhoods and small towns, there was a noticeable diminution in community connection and an increased personal isolation. Yet communities did form, and various common practices emerged to compensate for the losses: country clubs, community groups and organizations, activities revolving around children such as organized sports and schools. Friendships and relationships took on new forms and patterns as contemporary life recast itself in a new way.

Having lived in Archer City and Houston (among other places), McMurtry was acutely aware of the sweeping social transformation, and he explored the relationship of people to place yet again. Now the place was the tree-lined streets of suburban Houston, with its brick houses, sidewalks, local shopping marts, and sometimes confused people who negotiated their identity in a new and somewhat amorphous world. It is this new social dynamic that McMurtry considered in a sweeping but highly integrated trilogy that explores the conflicts, challenges, and hidden joys of contemporary life.

Moving On (1970)

Moving On is an intricate blend of subgenres. Under the broad umbrella of the social novel in the British tradition, McMurtry combined elements of the contemporary Western, the academic novel, and the novel of urbanity. The book is a lengthy exploration of the interior lives and exterior interactions of a series of young characters, particularly Patsy Carpenter and her husband, Jim. The couple is rather wealthy, and Jim moves from aspiration to aspiration, from photographer to graduate student to untitled functionary at IBM. In a rapidly changing social environment with shifting mores, Patsy tries to come into her own as she struggles with her malleable sense of identity and unpredictable emotional vicissitudes. *Moving On* shifts locales, beginning on the rodeo circuit as Jim explores photography. But the bulk of the novel is set in Houston, as Jim and a number of other colorful characters pursue graduate degrees at Rice University. These figures include Emma and Flap Horton as well-developed secondary characters (they become the central figures in *Terms of Endearment*). *Moving On* is fundamentally an exploration of a dynamic and changing social world, and the historical and geographical setting is tremendously important in clarifying the conflicts faced by a set of characters whose actions and motives might otherwise be incomprehensible. It is the early 1960s, at the beginning of a cultural revolution that none of the characters particularly anticipate. Especially in the city, there is an instability to social relationships that leads to a peculiar and mysterious emotional exhaustion that plagues the characters from the beginning. Beneath the joviality of their parties and smaller social gatherings there is an anxiety about the future. The normally confident Flap Horton nearly commits suicide for fear that he has failed his preliminary doctoral exams. Jim Carpenter cannot seem to find identity and satisfaction in any vocation. Emma Horton struggles to maintain some sense of family normalcy in the midst of it all, and the main character, Patsy, seemingly always on the verge of tears, must endure her own interior emotional unpredictability, which derives in part from her inability to discover a discrete and individual identity. John Leonard in the *New York Times*, though he questioned the scope, breadth, and even structure of the novel, noted the richness of the characterizations, calling the book "a novel of monumental honesty" and concluding that "attention must be paid."[2] Though early critics, including Leonard, questioned the novel's length and ponderous nature and expressed concern about its lack of plot, many were taken by the characters and their problems. As Leonard noted in the title of his review, it is without a doubt a novel of its times.

In a certain way, there is a deceptive structure to this lengthy and sprawling work. The narrative consists of four books of precisely twenty chapters each, all of them centered on Patsy Carpenter and her friends and other intimates. Book One, "The Beginning of the Evening," introduces Patsy and Jim as they travel the rodeo circuit pursuing Jim's temporary aspiration to be a rodeo photographer. In their travels, they meet and become friends with the aging rodeo clown Pete Tatum, other colorful rodeo figures, and the irascible rodeo hero and ladies' man Sonny Shanks. This portion of the narrative takes them from Texas and throughout the Southwest and north into Wyoming. It is full of description and a vivid exploration of the West as place, not only through its physical geography but through its indigenous and contemporary characters. Book Two, "Houston, Houston, Houston," brings Patsy and Jim to Rice University, where Jim, having given up on photography for a time, has enrolled in a Ph.D. program in English. This book explores the early development and devolution of their marriage and the interactions among graduate students, graduate student couples, and their professors, particularly the main professor, the ineffectual provocateur Bill Duffin. Patsy must try to understand her role as a wife and her identity as an individual in a world full of men who desire her sexually, even as they quietly admire her as a reader and a lay intellectual. Book Three, "Sleeping Around," centers around the birth and the first year of Patsy's child Davey; her affair with another graduate student, Hank; Jim's travels as a temporary photographer on movie sets; and his one-time dalliance with an aging prostitute. This portion of the narrative highlights the instability of each and every relationship, not just those of married couples but those involving friends and temporary lovers. Particular attention is paid to Patsy's unpredictable and shifting emotional reactions to situations she at least in part creates of her own volition. Book Four, "Summer's Lease," deals with the accidental yet somehow predictable death of Sonny Shanks, the slow dissolution of Patsy and Jim's marriage, and Patsy's successful attempt to rescue her sister, Miri, from a bad relationship and drug dependency. All this occurs as Patsy attempts to find herself as a complex contemporary world confronts her with a plethora of emerging choices that ironically challenge her ability to act with any force or agency, instead driving her to a condition of relative emotional and physical independence.

In a preface to a 1987 reprint of *Moving On*, McMurtry pondered his own creation and provided a clue regarding his motives in developing Patsy's character. He wrote: "The knottiest aesthetic problem I fumbled with in *Moving On* is whether its heroine, Patsy Carpenter, cries too much. I might say that I had not the even haziest consciousness of this problem while I was writing the book. Then it was published, and I immediately started finding myself locked into arguments with women, all of whom resented Patsy's tears" (5). Given the book's original year of publication, 1970, this reaction is a remarkable barometer of the times, as women of McMurtry's acquaintance seemed to resent not simply women's tears but the representation of a woman who was in essence of another time, a child of the 1940s and 1950s, with that era's social mores and highly gendered patterns of behavior. Patsy's frequent tears made her seem to them passé, even weak, her crying perhaps not appropriate to an era in which the long-standing feminist movement had taken on a new momentum and fervency. But McMurtry politely defended himself with a simple assertion of verisimilitude, claiming that most of the women he had known growing up were perpetually on the verge of tears.

In *Moving On*, it is not Patsy's tears that define her but her psychological density, intellectual strength, and emotional volatility and ultimate solidity, characteristics she clearly shares with the men in the novel, though they are defined more by exterior behavior than by interior reflection. In the same preface, McMurtry continued to elucidate the character he had created: "The book was written in the late sixties, and set less than a decade earlier. As arguments over Patsy's tears persisted, I gradually came to regard it as essentially a historical novel, one which attempted to describe a way of life—mainly, the graduate school way of life—in a vanished era. The era had only vanished a few years earlier, but it was definitively gone" (6). It is quite remarkable and indicative of the times that McMurtry would call a novel written in the relative present a "historical novel." The rapid social changes of the 1960s and 1970s had, according to the author, unintentionally rendered it so. But, in the manner that McMurtry writes, any great social novel is a work of social representation, and *Moving On* bears comparison to a number of nineteenth- and twentieth-century British and American novels of dense historical and cultural texture. In the social preoccupations and the psychological intricacy of its main character, *Moving On* particularly brings to mind George Eliot's *Middlemarch,* Emily Bronte's *Jane Eyre,* and the many city novels of Edith Wharton. McMurtry's particular contribution is to remind readers that the urban locales of his own Texas warrant the same treatment as those novels' settings.

In its blending of subgenre and by McMurtry's own admission, *Moving On* evokes the setting and conventions of the academic novel. Often novels of this variety deal with the machinations of academic politics and personalities, but McMurtry chose a more uncommon subject, the experiences of graduate students before they enter the profession, including their anxieties over their studies and their interaction with older professors, their often pretentious social gatherings, their youth, early marriages, and sexual dalliances. *Moving On* is often grave and emotionally intense, but there is always an undercurrent of wry humor, situational irony, and even parody, which is never more obvious than when the novel engages an academic context. Again, Patsy and Jim become a graduate student couple at Rice, befriend Emma and Flap Horton, and become more than casually acquainted with their major professor, Bill Duffin, a modernist scholar of apparently national reputation. Duffin remains with his wife, Lee, in an oddly functional marriage bereft of genuine intimacy, and he spends much of his time indiscriminately pursuing young women regardless of their marital status. Patsy, who is quite attractive, immediately draws his attention. But he is committed to his wife in a peculiar and mysterious way, and their relationship is a window into a rather comic conception of the academic and the academic life. Speaking to his wife late at night in bed, Duffin muses:

> "You certainly aren't faded now," Bill said. "Look, I've laid aside my book, and it's the best book on Joyce since the year before last. What more in the way of passion could you ask?"
>
> She took up her brush. "Would you even lay aside Joyce himself?"
>
> "Don't be coquettish," he said, turning on his bed light. "No modernist worth his salt would lay aside James Joyce for a woman. Lesser men, yes. In your present state of bloom I'd lay aside Ford Maddox Ford for you without a moment's hesitation." (545–546)

In his humor, Duffin is quite serious. He remains a committed scholar, yet there is a perpetual undercurrent of self-criticism and even self-abhorrence in his behavior and his words. He seems caught in a middle place between his genuine interest in his academic subject and his sneaking sense that it may have little meaning in the broader scheme of things. This problem is exacerbated by the fact that he is apparently nationally renowned, in some contexts deeply admired, and certainly a figure of authority and repute among his many students. His emotional weaknesses, his propensity to take advantage of his position with young women, and his underlying fear that he isn't worth all the fuss lead to a vaguely ironic posture that defines his character. His wife, Lee, seems (thought they never discuss it openly) to understand his rather pathetic plight and remains tolerant, even of his betrayals. Betrayal on both their parts is in fact at the core of their relationship, something they have come to accept without concern. Their situation, sad as it may be, elicits even from them as many chuckles as tears. They are more or less beyond tears. As an older couple, they offer a window into the future both for Patsy and Jim Carpenter and for Emma and Flap Horton. Their struggles (those of Flap and Emma are developed more later in the trilogy) are new and, as such, more grave and pressing. As the two male graduate students struggle in stops and starts to form an identity, they begin to see the future they will share with Bill Duffin. Particularly Patsy and Jim begin to experience marital troubles, in part because of Jim's split loyalties between his emerging sense of vocational identity and ego and his commitment to his wife. Patsy, a young woman, comes to realize her own emotional complexities and her sexual identity outside marriage. All of these apparent problems are in a certain ways peculiar to the middle and upper classes. None of the characters are genuinely plagued by the pressing concerns of poverty and want. In this sense, academia becomes a metonym for the lesser problems of the privileged, problems that for them are nevertheless real, painful, and in many ways insurmountable.

But *Moving On* is at its core a novel about Patsy Carpenter and, by extension, a work about the concerns and issues that confronted young middle-class women in the 1960s and 1970s. Though many voices and movements had attempted to deal with the plight of women in the modern world prior to this time, movements that culminated in women winning the right to vote, a new urgency about achieving equal rights, coupled with a scrutiny of male and female roles, had begun to catch on. Popular books such as Betty Friedan's *The Feminine Mystique* (1963) had taken particular aim at the cultural patterns that circumscribed women's roles in marriage through their representation in popular media. Economic circumstances, changing educational policies, and the basic needs of a postindustrial economy had begun to render these gender patterns unworkable and even absurd. It is within this social context that the novel takes on a pressing relevance, and Patsy's dynamic character becomes a powerful analog of the times. Yes, she cries frequently, and McMurtry later defended this on the grounds of observation. The many objections to her tears expressed by McMurtry's friends suggest not a negative aesthetic judgment but an ideological objection to a behavior no longer considered appropriate. This is in fact a component of her effectiveness as a fully drawn character. Initially, she behaves in direct accordance with the feminine mystique; she is childlike, dependent, expecting to play the confined role of the dependent woman. But as she develops over time and is conditioned by a new set of circumstances she can only vaguely apprehend, she slowly changes, in terms of both her emotional vicissitudes and her external behaviors. One major conflict that emerges as she tries to understand her role in marriage is sexual. She is not alone in this. Among the graduate students and professors at Rice, sexual flirtations and full-scale dalliances are common, even frequently the norm. Bill Duffin sets the tone with his somewhat cynical disregard for the proprieties of marriage. But McMurtry is clear as he enters the mind of each character that the sexual impulse is ubiquitous. Most if not all of the men are attracted to Patsy, and other indiscretions are more than common.

Sex in fact seems to be the primary preoccupation of this otherwise studious group of professors in training. But underneath the apparent folly of their behaviors is a sense that the very framework of marriage and the prescribed roles that define it are falling apart. The previous patterns still hold for the moment. Men are training to be professors while women support them, and the women are having children and taking on domestic responsibilities. Emma and Flap Horton are the primary examples of this behavior, as Flap studies for exams while Emma takes care of their growing brood. But the domestic myth is under siege as we see that the women are suited for more than domestic chores. Patsy Carpenter, Emma Horton, and Lee Duffin are by no means wallflowers or porcelain dolls ornamenting an ideal marriage. They are formidable interlocutors in a series of interchanges with their husbands in private. They prove to be intellectual partners and, at times, competitors. They read and are fully engaged in the intellectual life of the community, and they often have complex opinions themselves, even around the works their husbands are studying. The feminine mystique is clearly under siege, and as their husbands stray from them sexually, they no longer remain passive. McMurtry renders them as fully realized individuals with complex sexual identities.

Patsy begins this process of self-discovery early in the novel with a brief flirtation with the aging rodeo clown Pete Tatum, who in a touching moment places his hand on hers. Later, after the dissolution of her marriage, the two meet again and finally sleep together, much to the embarrassment of both. Patsy's initial naiveté is clear as she is playfully caught in an attempted seduction by the rodeo hero Sonny Shanks. In this interchange, she is appalled at Sonny's forwardness and casual confidence, and she appears childish and out of place. But as the novel proceeds, life and circumstances take over, and as her marriage begins to dissolve, even as she is pregnant she falls for one of the graduate students, Hank, and in the process undergoes not only a dramatic sexual awakening but a heartrending process of self-discovery that is more than intellectual but deeply psychological. In this context, McMurtry challenges the boundaries of generally accepted categories of love and commitment as her feelings for Jim and Hank take on a complexity that cannot be classified.

After discovering the affair, Jim accepts the situation and tries to recover their relationship. But the rift is too deep. He has himself strayed briefly, and she is unable to return to their former intimacy. He eventually leaves her, and she must survive emotionally as an individual. In this context, Hank is not enough. She is financially independent, a strong and willful mother, and increasingly independent even in the face of her own emotional needs and desires. The term "love" becomes inadequate to describe her feelings for the men in her life, and nothing can fully satisfy her until she comes to terms with her own inner fortitude. It is in this context that her final transformation occurs. After she has achieved emotional independence, she must rescue her sister, Miri, from the drug culture in California and from a degenerate boyfriend. After the two return home, Patsy becomes a kind of matriarch in a growing group of family members. Some of her confusion remains, but it is now the confusion of a normal, reasonably stable and independent human being. *Moving On* thus participates in the rich tradition of the social novel. It deals with Texas in its transformation from ranch culture to modernity and is a complex psychological novel that charts the circuitous yet progressive development of a woman negotiating her identity in a changing world.

All My Friends Are Going to Be Strangers (1972)

After writing *Moving On*, McMurtry quickly moved on to a novel that, as a prequel, was interestingly dissimilar in form. Sharing a number of ancillary characters with the earlier novel, *All My Friends Are Going to Be Strangers* further advances many of its themes and concerns but takes on a different tone and an increased emotional intensity. In the preface to the 2000 edition, written nearly thirty years after the book's initial publication, McMurtry provided some insight into his state of mind as he worked on the volume:

> I wrote this novel very rapidly; in a sense, I exhaled it. Another way to put it is that *Moving On*, written just previously, expelled it, as a kind of afterbirth.
> *Moving On* was a long effort, twenty-five hundred pages in manuscript, at least in the initial draft. As I approached the end I felt tired but also exhilarated; some energy remained beneath the fatigue, and a momentum that I didn't want to lose. Indeed, within the fatigue itself, there was a kind of high. (3)

The rich but loose and sprawling nature of *Moving On* culminates in a tightly structured and pared down narrative in *All My Friends Are Going to Be Strangers,* told from a focused and refined point of view. Although there is certainly humor in Patsy Carpenter's story, in the second novel satire and absurdist comedy shape the language and the main character's consciousness. The brief but compelling narrative continues the tensions of *Moving On,* with its settings moving in turn among Houston, San Francisco, and the barren landscapes of Texas and Mexico.

But *All My Friends Are Going to Be Strangers* is a kind of bildungsroman (or, more particularly, a kunstlerroman), and it actually inverts the characteristic purposes of a narrative designed to chart the coming of age of an artist (in this case a novelist). The main character, Danny Deck, moves from false self-knowledge to a full-blown conscious lack of understanding, from stability to instability. Like many of McMurtry's novels, *All My Friends Are Going to Be Strangers* deals with the complexity of the times through a style of unreserved intensity, as human relationships, particularly romantic and sexual ones, are as transient and unstable as the social institutions that confine and protect them. In the *New York Times Book Review,* Jim Harrison commented on the novel's tone and thematic tension:

> It is difficult to characterize a talent as outsized as McMurtry's. Often his work seems disproportionately sensual and violent, but these qualities in "All My Friends Are Going to Be Strangers" are tempered by his comic genius, his ability to render a sense of landscape and place, and an interior intellectual tension that resembles in intensity that of Saul Bellow's "Mr. Sammler's Planet." McMurtry will flash back and forth between the splendidly brilliant and the sloppily inane but has a sense of construction and proper velocity that always saves him. McMurtry has the faults of a strong but careless writer like Mailer, but they are easily forgiven in this particular novel, which seems so thoroughly a type of "American" classic without any of the painless charm of housebroken literature.[3]

The novel is a trim narrative of eighteen chapters told from the point of view of Danny Deck, who is introduced as a new figure in the elaborate weave of characters in the Houston novels. The story takes place a few years before the events in *Moving On,* when Flap Horton is an undergraduate and before he and his wife, Emma, have children. Danny is a fellow undergraduate at Rice University and a budding novelist who has sold his first book to Random House and to a Hollywood studio. In spite of his success, Danny is confused by a series of complicated relationships with women, including his pregnant wife, Sally, who is harsh, indifferent, and often cruel; his middle-aged neighbor Jenny Salomea; Emma Horton, who represents a kind of stability and normalcy he craves; and his eccentric sometime girlfriend, Jill. This peculiar matrix of relationships sends Danny into a vortex of confusion and emotional turbulence, as he attempts to find vocational and personal identity in a series of moves that contrast in vivid terms the worlds of Houston, San Francisco, and rural Texas. The novel is a loving parody of the coming-of-age novel, quietly skeptical of the very process of identity formation, and at times employs elements of absurdist comedy as self-knowledge for its central character becomes as elusive as place.

At least from the Thalia saga forward, there is a comic element present in McMurtry's novels, and in this middle period, with this trim novel, he was focused and fairly directed toward an absurdist vision. There is instability in Danny's world that has him constantly spinning from place to place, from relationship to relationship. His intentions are constantly thwarted, and he seems oddly unable to appreciate the positive things that have happened to him, including his mercurial publishing success. McMurtry seemed to deliberately eschew the philosophical intensity central to 1950s absurdist theatre or even to the work of postmodern contemporaries such as Thomas Pynchon. While these other artists took the absurd to the extreme and dealt more thoroughly with the failure of language, McMurtry's sense of the absurd was more experiential, less rooted in existentialism, and more centered on the simple inability of humans to the control the social and other circumstances that buffet them from place to place, mood to mood. In a scene involving Danny and his sometime friend the aging sociology professor Godwin, he describes a circumstance where a gesture of conventional heroism is thwarted and results not in tragedy but in a darkly comic scene. Traveling across Texas, they are caught in a flash flood, and Godwin sees a trapped bus and attempts to help:

> Godwin arrived at that time, to everyone's consternation. The fat woman screamed. One of the dogs immediately swam toward him, menacingly. Godwin lost his nerve and swam back a little way, pursued by the sinister wet dog. The goats didn't like him either. He began to swim after the drowning chickens, but the chickens were long gone. One tiny man got on top of the bus and pulled at the fat woman's hand, while the other stayed in the water and pushed on her ass. The young woman had managed to get on the top of the bus and was nursing her baby. The clouds broke open at that moment and the bright West Texas sun shone over the desert. (76)

The absurd certainly has a long history, with its roots in Greek Menippean satire and later in the comic and stock characters of Shakespeare. But this scene suggests the more recent influence, acknowledged by absurdists such as Samuel Beckett and Eugene Ionesco, that is, the vaudevillian stage and the short films of the silent era featuring Charlie Chaplin and Buster Keaton. The scene McMurtry orchestrates is organized around physicality and movement, and the comedy centers on a lone figure that begins with a serious intent, only to be subverted by a chaotic and ridiculous world that sends him into a hilarious devolution of purpose and meaning. The scene is in many ways a crystallized image of Danny's circumstances throughout the novel, as he moves from place to place, seeking meaning and value in relationships, only to find himself floundering outside them in a world that in many ways doesn't make sense. He quits school, leaves his wife, who is unconcerned about his departure, and finds momentary solace with the Hollywood artist Jill, who for unexplainable reasons cannot provide him with the emotional and physical intimacy he desires. He wanders back to Texas, momentarily stopping at an uncle's ranch, only to be insulted and ridiculed, and finally stumbles into Emma Horton's bed, only to find that the ideal vision she represents can never be his. We see this absurdist vision captured as he contemplates his identity as a writer: "Until I moved to California, I hadn't met many writers. . . . I knew a couple of journalists who planned to knock off and write novels some day, but I couldn't count them as real writers either . . . the only person I knew who actually published anything was old man Sickles who had written a booklet on driver training. One of the reasons I couldn't tell whether I was a real writer or not was because I had no one authentic to compare myself to" (84).

From the inception of the novel, Danny is a success. He is published. The studios are enthusiastic about adapting his work. He has been given tens of thousands of dollars and has been offered the opportunity to write the screenplay for his novel. But, even so, he has little confidence as a writer because he doesn't trust the unpredictable, seemingly insane world that has designated him as one. In the end, he loses faith in the ability of words to capture the essences of his experience, as he literally drowns his second manuscript in the shallow waters of the Rio Grande. The absurdist theme of the futility of language informs Danny's last dramatic gesture, and the novel concludes not with the realization of the artist's purpose, typical of the kunstlerroman, but with the artist alone and more alienated from his identity than he was before.

The figure of the artist is McMurtry's particular concern in *All My Friends Are Going to Be Strangers*. Some circumstances are changed for fictional purposes, but the trajectory of Danny's emergence as a writer roughly parallels McMurtry's own. Danny, then, can be read as a kind of alter ego for McMurtry, and the novel can be seen as the story of his early development as an author. The artist's role is not one that McMurtry is entirely comfortable with, as he confesses in the preface:

> His [Danny Deck's] dilemma was one most artists face and struggle with at some point, usually as inconclusively as Danny himself does: whether art

can be persuaded to allow its artists a little normal life and common happiness and yet permit them to create.

Danny's bleak conclusion is that art won't be persuaded—not really; not "normal" life, as exemplified for him by Emma Horton and her solidly normal kitchen. (3)

McMurtry identifies himself with Danny, at least indirectly, saying, "He wasn't me, but there was no large gap between his sensibility and my own. I became comfortable with his voice at once and liked his quirks and his mainly sad appreciation for the absurd" (3). The common question of whether the artist is himself "normal" or can be expected to live "normally" is coupled ambiguously with the question of whether art itself has value in an absurd world.

Danny's book is referred to vaguely and appears to be similar in content to McMurtry's first novel, *Horseman, Pass By.* That first serious and somewhat idealist venture into the changing texture of modernity has little in common with *All My Friends Are Going to Be Strangers,* since it is a serious inquiry into the positive if incomplete development of its young protagonist in a world where ethics seem to have some meaning and relevance. In the later novel, Danny's world seems to lack any moral urgency, as the exhausted emotions of its characters lead them to mysteriously dysfunctional or at least mildly dissipated lives. The artist's efforts, then, to sacrifice normalcy in an attempt to make sense of this world are fraught with difficulty, and the tradeoff is highly questionable. Danny's final state of mind involves an ironically irrational response that at the same time makes sense in a world that is perplexing and strange. McMurtry concludes in the preface that Danny in some way lives on, presumably as a writer, but in the context of this novel one must wonder how he adapts finally to his role as an artist. Unlike in the traditional kunstlerroman, he doesn't come to any positive realization of his role as creator, nor does he adapt and accept his role as an alienated but purposeful artist. Thus, the artist and his work must stand in perpetual tension, and the sacrifice of either one for the other remains a problematic choice.

From a social and historical standpoint, Danny's story involves a series of movements, and, as a novel primarily concerned with urban and suburban Houston, *All My Friends Are Going to Be Strangers* explores its subject through a series of contrasts. Much like other novels in the tradition of the social novel, *All My Friends Are Going to Be Strangers* makes a strident sociological claim, arguing for the influence of place on the development of personal identity. Danny's confusion is certainly personal, but it is also caused by the instability and confusion of modernity. This has in part been McMurtry's concern from the beginning, as the decline of range culture and the birth of the city and the rise of the oil economy are central in *Horseman, Pass By* and *Leaving Cheyenne*. But the Houston novels take us further into the future, are less concerned with the specific contrast of oil and range, and are more focused on the troubling and tension-ridden parallels between the east and the west (California and Texas), the city and the landscape, home and the alienating world of the foreign and strangely incomprehensible cityscapes of Los Angeles and San Francisco. Danny quits school, leaves his pregnant wife (with her encouragement) to go to Los Angeles to see his novel's adaptation into film, and ultimately finds himself in San Francisco. He leaves because his marriage is failing. His wife, Sally, wants a baby more than a husband, and she is quite willing to see him go, initiating his departure with apparent intention by having an affair. Danny becomes disillusioned with his undergraduate studies, and, though he will miss his friends Flap and Emma Horton, he quietly hopes to find some stability elsewhere. Ironically, although his practical success in Los Angeles seems to come easily, Danny's indefinable loneliness and growing lack of purpose become acute. He is offered the opportunity to write the screenplay for his book and is given money enough to live a privileged life, even as he works on his second novel for Random House. But his personal life continues to spin out of control. By chance, he meets the commercial artist Jill, but, in this situation and for reasons that are never fully made clear, Jill will not consummate or solidify their relationship and eventually leaves.

Danny has all the success a young man could want, but what he really craves is the "normalcy" that is represented by Emma Horton and her kitchen. But the apparently conventional relationship of Flap and Emma is an anomaly in a world that is defined by shifting social arrangements, and Danny must struggle to live and create in an environment that offers no genuine stability in human relationships. The characters in this ever-changing social context must perpetually struggle with identity, loneliness, alienation, and the results of their own confused dissipation. Danny's problem is that he takes things seriously, unlike people such as Sally and Godwin, who seem to have adapted by embracing the absurdity of both circumstances and themselves. It is this seriousness that gives the novel an underlying tonality of hope. Danny's final gesture seems on one hand a sign of his growing emotional instability and on the other a sign of agency, and he finally makes a choice and seems ready to take on the world with all of its complexities. For McMurtry, Danny lives on, and we can safely assume successfully, perhaps even in some loose way as McMurtry himself. He will live in some ways in isolation, but he will create characters that remain comic and deeply sympathetic and will transcend the absurdist contexts within which they live. We might assume that Danny will write stories that revive the Western past, tales of both dissipation and heroism, embellished stories about historical figures such as William Bonny and Calamity Jane, fictional novels such as those of the *Lonesome Dove* saga that redefine the heroic in a stark naturalistic context. We might also consider that he will continue and further develop the life of Duane Moore from *The Last Picture Show,* which culminates in a hard-won self-knowledge and contentment that elude Danny in his youth. In this sense, McMurtry attempts to delicately balance the absurd with the ostensibly "normal," as his characters painfully but at least partially cope with a dynamic and ever-shifting modern world.

Terms of Endearment (1975)

The Houston novels reach their apogee with *Terms of Endearment,* a sweetly ironic and tragic tale that continues to emphasize themes of spiritual and psychological displacement, lost love, failed relationships, and, ultimately, death. But amid these realities, blended with all the dissipation and quiet despair of the characters, is a sense of tenderness and unity that appears in the relationship of a mother and a daughter and in the many men who surround them. The novel continues with the character of Emma Horton, who is portrayed as a common, barely attractive, but deeply human young woman full of desire and self-doubt, hope and indefinable need. But central to the novel is her mother, Aurora Greenway, a forty-nine-year-old widow of fairly independent means who can still play the coquette to a host of suitors. She is moderately wealthy, cultured, and in her own way emotionally self-sufficient. But at the same time she gains much pleasure and even emotional sustenance from the many relationships she maintains but keeps at arm's length. She is a consummate wit, full of humor and irony. With her (to borrow from Shakespeare), every word stabs, and yet those people who have become in various ways enraptured with her keep coming back for more. The novel is best described as an endearing and loving satire, one that deals primarily with a mother and a daughter, in a relationship that is tight and dependable but comically dysfunctional. The overall story explores human co-dependency as the norm, and human fallibility serves in an odd way to strengthen the relationships depicted. At the same time, the novel is a tragedy, as it concludes with the unexpected and early death of Emma, charting the intimate psychological process by which she comes to terms with her fate.

Terms of Endearment met with mixed reviews, many quite similar in the concerns expressed to the reviews for *Moving On.* The critics' primary issue, even though the later novel is fairly brief, was with form, structure, and plot. Some reviewers were more critical than others. In the *New York Times Book Review,* Robert Towers seemed perplexed, writing that the novel remains "underdeveloped" and "lost among many distractions," and finally concluded:

"Reflecting McMurtry's earlier achievements, one would like to think that the author is taking large risks, that he is deliberately rupturing his tone and collapsing his structure in order to achieve a richer complexity or something like that. But the evidence does not support such a wish."[4] Towers's concern with structure echoes the thoughts of critics of other McMurtry novels, though Towers registers some awareness of the character nuance that seems to be novel's primary locus of concern. In the *New York Times,* Christopher Lehmann-Haupt expressed a similar judgment but was more forgiving, acknowledging the features of the genre that in many ways justify the structure:

> I would speculate that Mr. McMurtry has taken leftover parts of several novels and combined them to make a machine not unlike what they display on television to make the point that a certain bank will buy any car you fancy. The form of "Terms of Endearment" looks no less ridiculous.
>
> And yet, like that car, the novel runs. One laughs at the slapstick, one weeps at the maudlin, and one likes all of Mr. McMurtry's characters, no matter how delicately or broadly they are drawn. . . . So it must be that Mr. McMurtry has something special going for him. He can write up a mess and still win you over with it.[5]

What is most telling about these judgments and what might in some way qualify them is the commonality and fundamental truth they convey: McMurtry seems uninterested in creating a narrative that makes sense. The novel's lack of direction mirrors his primary preoccupation, the directionless nature of human character development and growth as well as the strangely amorphous contours of the modern urban experience. The form of the novel is not unlike that found in many of the most well-loved farces, and the situations and circumstances in *Terms of Endearment* certainly extend satire and irony to the point of the farcical, though the novel's conclusion undercuts this tone significantly. Still, over time and in later considerations, it is Lehmann-Haupt's more sympathetic perspective that has seemed to dominate, and the novel, with some modifications to the story in the screenplay, was adapted into a film in 1983, directed by James L. Brooks and starring Shirley MacLaine and Debra Winger in the roles of Aurora Greenway and Emma Horton. The film won five Academy Awards, including Best Picture, among many other accolades.

Though the narrator only alludes to the affair, the story begins after Emma Horton's tryst with Danny Deck. The first part takes place in the early 1960s. It deals with the relationship between Emma and Aurora but in many ways centers on the latter. Aurora is sharp, biting, ironic in her sensibilities, and playful if somewhat cruel to those around her. Again, she has many suitors, all of whom she maintains but keeps at a safe distance. These suitors are by no means bereft of accomplishment, which speaks significantly to Aurora's appeal as a potential wife. They include the retired army commander General Scott; Trevor Waugh, a wandering yachtsman who is as wealthy as he is bereft of purpose; an Italian merchant and former opera singer; and Vernon Dalhart, an oilman with a talent for making money who lives in his car on top of a parking lot he owns. The narrative is largely plotless and is not easily divided into discrete episodes. Instead, it meanders in a remarkably lifelike way, centering on the sadly comic exploits of its many characters.

Aurora calls her daughter daily, demanding her attention at a moment's notice while being seemingly indifferent to it. She has a close and edgy relationship with her longtime maid, Rosie, and she spends her days sleeping, reading, cooking, going to lunches, making dinners for her suitors, and dispensing with them at will. In a parallel and more serious plot, Emma struggles with her marriage to the hapless Flap Horton, who began his academic career with great promise but who barely earns tenure and eventually moves them to Nebraska to take a job as department chair at a smaller university. In a minor but sadly hilarious subplot, Rosie must deal with her wandering husband, Royce, who tires of Rosie after decades and finds himself with another woman, only to become angry when Rosie decides to go to a dance with General Scott's chauffeur. The novel is divided into two parts of disparate length. The first part, "Emma's Mother," comprises nineteen chapters that deal with Aurora and her exploits and with her endearing if peculiar relationship with Emma, as well as with the tragicomic troubles of Rosie and Royce Dunlup. The second part, "Mrs. Greenway's Daughter, 1971–1976," is a brief section containing one lengthy chapter and is much more serious, portraying the disillusion of Emma's marriage to Flap and her final battle with the cancer that takes her life. The pairing of the comic and the tragic adds a strangely deterministic quality to the novel's thematic texture, as characters live for a future that tends sadly to elude them.

Terms of Endearment, like the other Houston novels, continues to make a theme of setting, focusing on the lives and the complex and often comic interactions of a series of characters deeply embedded in the social texture of the city and the suburbs. They are shaped by this context in ways they don't fully comprehend, and, as adapted as they are to their world, much of their angst is created and intensified by the environment in which they live. Confusion is the order of the day. There is confusion with respect to identity, the future, the workability of social relationships, and self-knowledge. Aurora and Emma seem constantly to be seeking and not finding, desperately and comically looking for something that has been lost or never existed. Neither struggles financially. On the contrary, Aurora especially has a fine house, no need to work, a maid, a couple of fine works of art (including a Renoir) hanging on her wall. Emma, though not as well off as her mother, is comfortably middle class, with children and a husband who is (at least initially) a well-respected graduate student and later a professor of literature. Their mutual malaise stems from something deeper, more endemic to the times, more a feature of contemporary, even postmodern American middle-class life.

Their wants are pressing but indefinable, their needs deeply psychological and sometimes even hidden. Their concerns are in fact mirrored by McMurtry in the environment itself. One night, Vernon, the uneducated but successful oil magnate who has the Midas touch in his business, sits in his well-apportioned Lincoln at night at the top of the multilevel parking structure he owns. After meeting and being taken by Aurora, he looks out over the city at night:

> He went out and stood by the wall a while, popping his knuckles rapidly to make up for all of the time he had restrained himself. Two or three planes went over, but he scarcely noticed them. He looked down at the city and after some study was able to figure out almost exactly where her house was. River Oaks was mostly just a patch of darkness because the tall thick trees hid the streetlights, but he knew its perimeters and worked himself north from Westheimer until he located where he thought Aurora must be. He heard the phone ringing in the Lincoln but didn't answer it. (160)

Vernon's line of vision allows him to see more than the outlines of the city. He sees River Oaks and Westheimer and the patterned trees that cover the street-lights. He certainly sees the outline of the avenues and boulevards that form the intricate social maze that was the American suburb in the late 1960s. As he stares across the suburban landscape at night, he ponders his own confusion as he thinks about his surprisingly powerful feelings toward Aurora. He is an oilman, unsophisticated, familiar with the rural regions from which he has extracted his wealth. But ironically it is men like him who have helped to create the modern city that has in its own way shaped the identity of the vexing and captivating woman he is coming to love. Though in part its creator, he is not a man of the city or the suburbs, and with a certain comic eccentricity he has quietly refused to allow himself to be absorbed by his surroundings. But, sadly and in some sense inevitably, it is love that draws him it.

Aurora, originally a product of Boston, is a creature of the city and the sub-urbs. Her days are spent lounging around her house, taking lunches with suit-ors, calling her daughter, hosting dinners and small parties. This is her world, a structured and oddly purposeless chaos reflected metaphorically in Vernon's nighttime vision: ordered, patterned, planned, yet built to no great or meaning-ful purpose beyond the daily, somewhat trite lives of its inhabitants. Yet there is an endearing pathos to those lives. Each person seeks meaning and finds it in daily relationships. Emma and Aurora are clearly dependent upon one another, regularly feeling the impulse to pick up the phone and expecting the other to drop whatever she may be doing to take the call, no matter how unimportant. Emma quietly longs for the indefinable feeling she had with Danny Deck, but she remains committed to Flap Horton and her children, even later in the novel after the disillusion of their relationship and their mutual infidelities. Aurora has formed an unconventional sisterhood with her maid, Rosie, who does her job but speaks to her employer with an informal lack of reverence, knowing she herself is more than an employee, which is proved when she leaves for a time and is not so quietly compelled by Aurora to return. Finally, there is a peculiar kind of co-dependency between Aurora and her many male admirers, who return to court her even after she playfully and frequently dashes their hopes. As an urban and suburban novel, *Terms of Endearment*, then, embodies the seeming purposelessness of postmodern suburban living, infused with a deep sense of its human texture and personal substance and combining parody and pathos in an intricate blend.

The novel's apparent plotlessness has another likely purpose: in many ways to advance the form of the novel of manners. This is perhaps true of all the novels in the Houston Trilogy, but *Terms of Endearment* embodies in specific ways the tradition of the social novel in the British and, later, the American traditions. In McMurtry's hands, the point is more or less exclusively to explore the complexities of human relationships and human psychology in a realist context, and that realism necessitates that the narrative be devoid of artificial structure or form. The focal point of that exploration is Aurora, her preoccupations and actions, and particularly her verbal manner and sensibility, both of which involve a kind of ironic distance and wit. Indeed, it is her words that bring her to life, her many interchanges with those who attend her. These quips and jibes are dispersed throughout the novel. The narrative begins with an echo, interestingly, of one of the most important novels in the tradition of the genre, Leo Tolstoy's *Anna Karenina*. That novel begins with a statement about what makes a happy marriage, and *Terms of Endearment* begins with Aurora saying, "The success of a marriage invariably depends upon the woman" (11). What follows is the first of many tense but playful conversations between Aurora and her daughter, in which Aurora displays her propensity for biting interchange.

"I hope he's persuaded you to diet," Aurora said. "No one should be so intractable as to reject the advice of their physician. Dr. Ratchford has had long years of experience and except where I'm concerned it's been my observation that his advice is invariably good. The sooner you start to diet the happier person you'll be."

"Why do you always make an exception of yourself?" Emma asked.

"Because I know myself best," Aurora said serenely. "I certainly wouldn't allow a physician to know me this well." (15)

Aurora is never quite serious, and what characterizes her is that she perpetually speaks what she believes to be the truth with a force that is double edged. On the one hand, she is strong willed and convinced of her rightness on all or most matters. There is little self-doubt or equivocation when she expresses an opinion. But she frequently undermines the force of her assertions with irony and sardonic humor. These interactions are typical of her and Emma, and she behaves in a similar way with everyone she encounters. Emma responds to her with the comfortable anger and frustration of a daughter who is close to her mother, and as such Emma is more forceful and combative in response. But most others, with the possible exception of Rosie, are driven to a frustrated silence. What typifies her relationships with the people around her and what becomes clear in her verbal manner is her seeming carelessness with regard to each of them. Oddly, she is quite dependent on Emma, Rosie, and her suitors collectively. They are part of the texture of a life that largely satisfies her. But, with regard to the suitors individually, they matter little. On the surface, to Aurora, life is a matter of simple and superficial enjoyment, and though she never expresses herself in overtly philosophical terms, she courts a kind of healthy absurdism, taking enjoyment where it presents itself.

She is a times preoccupied with aging, and when Rosie leaves for a time, it becomes clear that Aurora is emotionally dependent upon her. But these dependencies never thwart her basic sense of life as a human comedy, farcical in nature, and she sees herself as one of its major players. But there is a more serious side to her psychology, revealed by the third-person narrator: "Her inward motions no one seemed to see. What frightened her was the knowledge of how much she had already learned not to count on, how much she could do without. If her inward motion was not checked she had the feeling she would find herself beyond everyone, and that was the cause of the strangeness, which seemed to have chosen a physical place inside her, behind her breastbone. She could press hard against her chest and feel it, like a lump almost, a lump that sometimes nothing seemed to loosen" (149).

The feeling of strangeness is something that frequently comes over her, and though she is relatively secure financially, she still experiences a certain anxiety when it comes time to deal with money matters. But this strangeness runs deeper than the practical. She is comfortable in her daily life, in her home among her things, and she has a complicated relationship with people. She enjoys them but keeps them at a safe distance, and there is a tension between her natural independence and her recognition that emotional isolation can be mysteriously destructive. She seems unable to reconstitute her basic nature, and much of her humor is a shield against a hidden anxiety. Independence and self-sufficiency itself are things she fears, things that seem to drive her "inward motion," and she is very much its captive. This is the peculiar irony in her character, that within her levity there is a depth of emotion and a psychological remove from the human community that she vaguely understands as problematic. She cannot predict the consequences of her basic nature, how her emotional separation from people will affect her physically and mentally as she grows older. This interior psychology, recognizable and intricately drawn by the narrator, blends with the interactions of character to embody the basic ingredients and motives of the social novel and the novel of manners, a genre whose psychological intricacies are often underrated.

But in spite of the novel's farcical nature, in Book Two *Terms of Endearment* takes an unexpected and dramatic turn. Emma is diagnosed with cancer, and she must cope with the slow but inevitable recognition that she will die. McMurtry maintains the psychological complexity and intimacy, through the objective narrator, that were usually employed to explore Aurora, but now it is Emma's thoughts and moods that are the focus of concern. Initially, she goes through the expected anxieties and fears association with her condition, but, as she becomes sicker and as her body weakens, her thoughts become unpredictable, as McMurtry attempts to chart the natural process by which a human mind responds to the fact of death. She has many emotions, but much of what she feels reflects what appears to be a common and peculiarly calm resignation:

> In two months she found she had almost forgotten ordinary non-hospital life; perhaps the drugs had affected her memory, because she couldn't re-member it clearly enough to yearn for it. Sometimes it occurred to her that she was through with most things—sex, for instance, yet the thought didn't hurt much. It bothered her worse that she couldn't go Christmas shopping, for she was a person who loved Christmas. . . . Once, picking up a copy of the *Iliad* that Melba had given her, she chanced upon the phrase "among the dead," and found it comforting. Even counting people she knew, there were a lot of dead to be among: her father, for one, and a school chum who had been killed in a car wreck, and Sam Burns, and, she guessed, Danny Deck, the friend of her youth. She supposed him dead, though no one really knew. (402–403)

At this point what is most noticeable is her lack of fear and her seemingly natural acceptance. She ponders that it may be drug induced, but the trajectory of her thoughts seems clear and precise.

She later considers the possibility of going home for a time, and the prospect is anxiety provoking and unappealing. The sterile nature of the hospital brings her an odd comfort, and the familiarity of home would only strengthen her attachment to life, to her children and to the daily objects of home that are in a strange way life's fundamental substance. Most of the time, she feels herself "floating" between consciousness and oblivion, between life and death, and she takes a certain calm from reflecting upon the community of the dead, those she has been close to and those she has vaguely known. Though she is sometimes in pain, she has passed through a certain phase in the psychological process of coping, and as she comes to terms with her passing, McMurtry explores in detail the strange manner in which the body and the mind interact as both move toward the end. Emma moves in and out of self-awareness, and she achieves comfort ironically by unexpected things: the sterile hospital, the behavior of the staff as they seem quietly to accept her demise. In spite of all of this, she is acutely aware of the practical issue her death will cause. She knows her children cannot comprehend what is happening and as such will have regrets as they grow older. Emma has the presence of mind to tell them that she knows they love her. One might expect that her most forthright statement might be an expression of love for them, but she understands the complexities of regret and knows what they genuinely need to hear. In this sense, as the novel moves abruptly from the satirical and farcical to the dramatic and tragic, it never loses its density of psychological insight, as interior thoughts are integrated with external expression. In *Terms of Endearment,* then, McMurtry displays his deep familiarity with the literary tradition he spent much time studying, as he effectively integrates disparate genres in a novel that reflects a genuine advancement of the social novel in the realist tradition. The novel is in many ways a reflection of an era, as it deals with the satisfactions and dissatisfactions of people coping with the most commonplace manifestation of modernity, the modern city and suburb. Marriage seems a thing doomed to frequent failure and difficulty. Sexual infidelity seems an inevitable characteristic of life and sex itself a peculiar distraction from boredom and ennui. But in capturing all this, *Terms of Endearment* and, indeed, all the novels of the Houston Trilogy[6] bring people to life, making meaningful the setting in which they struggle, and each work illuminates the complex thoughts and consciousness of a group of recognizable human beings as they live, breathe, and, with a clumsy pathos, find their way.

CHAPTER 5

The *Lonesome Dove* Saga

The Pulitzer Prize–winning *Lonesome Dove* (1986) and its prequels, *Dead Man's Walk* (1995) and *Comanche Moon* (1997), as well as its sequel, *Streets of Laredo* (1993), perhaps represent McMurtry's signature achievement. Working both within and outside the Western, the most popular genre in American literature and film, in these books McMurtry developed characters that resonate in the consciousness of millions of readers and television viewers, even in a time when the Western has declined somewhat in popularity. Throughout his work, McMurtry has alternated between past and present, and he engages history even in novels set in the contemporary moment. His works have always been fairly popular, even though he never seems to compromise his artistic purpose. This tension in his fiction is never more present than in his greatest Westerns, particularly *Lonesome Dove* and the novels that follow in the series.

In 1981 McMurtry delivered a speech titled "Ever a Bridegroom: Reflections of a Failure" at the Fort Worth Art Museum. He considered the literary culture in Texas and pondered its inadequacies, angering many in the region. As a part of that talk, he mounted a scathing critique of the Western genre, arguing that it had exhausted itself and that its overtly mythic representations were historically inaccurate, calling it "Country and Western literature." His antipathy to the Western myth has been expressed repeatedly. In an interview with the *New York Times,* McMurtry said that the Western is a "romanticization" and argued that "the flaws in the structure are rarely described," stating emphatically that "I don't think these myths do justice to the richness of human possibility."[1] But it was perhaps inevitable that he would engage the genre with his own unique perspective. The early works and the Thalia novels were preoccupied with the history of Texas, particularly the transition in modes of living from the nineteenth to the twentieth century. Ranch culture was an interest never far from his consciousness, and major figures, both mythic and historical, did not escape his scrutiny. But the "alternative" or antimythic Western has a long history, especially in film, and this strand of the genre is noted for presenting heroes that at times appear villainous or at least overtly self-serving. Emerging out of the cultural crisis of the Vietnam and post-Vietnam eras, these stories effectively dismantle the hero figure that provided the primary ideological justification for the American imperialist project.[2]

In the *Lonesome Dove* saga read carefully, McMurtry is quite sympathetic to this revisionist idea. But he treats the genre with a measured sympathy, understanding it as the American morality play. As such, he presents characters who both embody and challenge the myth, rising above it in their essential humanity and likability but emerging as deeply flawed and only marginally redeemable. As human beings they are sensitive and vulnerable; as mythic figures they demonstrate a certain measured strength, but they are also representative men, and what can never be ignored is that they are the unwitting vanguard of modernity as they advance and defend the civilization that will destroy their own way of life. In all of this, McMurtry is careful not to create a one-sided critique of American westward expansion; Native Americans, particularly Comanches, are represented as often brutal and malevolent. Thus, the *Lonesome Dove* saga in its totality involves a remarkable blend of the comic, epic, and tragic modes. It embodies history while transcending it in a deep and aesthetically nuanced exploration of the human propensity for greed and violence, even as it affirms human virtues that are not simply mythic but universal.

Lonesome Dove (1986)

This grand novel begins the saga near the end of the story, as two retired Texas Rangers and some surviving members of their former troop manage the struggling Hat Creek Cattle Company on the Texas-Mexico border south of San Antonio. The novel is in many ways a synthesis of the themes McMurtry had developed over twenty-five years: the interrelationship of past and present, transience, the cruel indifference of history, the poignant human dilemma that continues as individuals seek place in a region that persistently changes before their eyes. The novel, with little dissent, was widely and positively reviewed, winning the Pulitzer Prize and quickly being adapted into a television miniseries that aired on CBS beginning February 5, 1989. The film drew twenty-six million viewers and arguably revived a genre that was waning significantly. Directed by Simon Wincer with a teleplay by Bill Wittliff, it garnered eighteen Emmy nominations and eight Emmy Awards, interestingly not including Best Miniseries. However, it won two Golden Globes, for Best Miniseries and

Best Actor (Robert Duvall, who played Augustus McRae opposite Tommy Lee Jones's Woodrow F. Call).

Subsequently, the film achieved even greater popularity and acclaim, spawning a series of sequels. It is perhaps revealing of the genuine content of the novel that, though present in the film, McMurtry's revisionist sensibilities were missed by many viewers. *Dead Man's Walk, Streets of Laredo,* and *Comanche Moon* were ultimately adapted into miniseries as well, but what appeared first was *Return to Lonesome Dove,* an ill-conceived attempt to take the characters in an overtly mythic direction that undercuts the darker themes of the novel and its film adaptation. Again, the novel itself achieved widespread acclaim. In the *Los Angeles Times Book Review,* John Horn called *Lonesome Dove* McMurtry's "loftiest novel, a wondrous work, drowned in love, melancholy, and yet, ultimately, exultant."[3] Recognizing the cinematic potential of the novel, many critics referred to the book as highly visual and cinematic, and they seemed equally captivated by the novel's stylistic simplicity and reserve, coupled with its exuberant romanticism. But they were acutely aware that, as a Western, *Lonesome Dove* was participating in something new.[4]

Lonesome Dove is first and foremost a work of fiction, an epic account of an iconic American story—the cattle drive. The characters are primarily of McMurtry's own making. But the author borrowed elements of plot from an actual history. The main characters, Woodrow F. Call and Augustus McRae, are based on Charles Goodnight (1836–1929) and Oliver Loving (1812–1867). Charles Goodnight ultimately became one of the most well-known cattle ranchers of the era. Early in life, he joined the Texas militia and, like Call and McCrae, the Texas Rangers, leading the posse that led to the recapture of Cynthia Ann Parker, who had been taken by the Comanche as a child and was assimilated and married to a local chief, Peta Nocona. Along with his friend and business partner Oliver Loving, Goodnight became a rancher, and together the two established the Goodnight-Loving Trail, which stretched from Texas into Colorado. Perhaps the most moving sequence in *Lonesome Dove* is the scene in which Augustus McCrae is attended at his death by Woodrow Call, who promises to deliver his friend's body back to Texas. This scene is based largely on circumstances involving Goodnight and Loving and their third cattle drive into the north. The location is different, but the events are precisely the same. As in the novel, Loving traveled ahead of the herd and was ambushed by Native Americans (an unnamed northern tribe in the novel but in actuality a group of Comanche). He was wounded by arrows; he sent his scout back to Goodnight and his men and escaped, only to die of gangrene at Goodnight's side. In response to a promise, Goodnight had Loving's body transported back to Texas and by the best accounts personally accompanied it. Again McCrae and Call are largely of McMurtry's making, but this and other events are drawn from the factual record including, interestingly, the character of Joshua Deets. The marker that Call carves for Deets after his death is based upon an epitaph Goodnight created late in life for Bose Ikard (1840s–1929), a former slave who worked for Goodnight for many years. As a historical figure, Goodnight appears by name briefly in all four novels in the saga, though he would have been too young to encounter the fictional characters in *Dead Man's Walk*. McMurtry may have chosen to include him to give a certain verisimilitude to the novels as a whole, but it is also likely that he wanted to emphasize that Augustus McCrae and Woodrow Call are creatures of fiction rather than thinly veiled renderings of historical figures.

Lonesome Dove itself is a sweeping narrative, epic in scope, told in the third-person omniscient in 102 chapters including interlaced narrative strands that relate and ultimately come together. The primary narrative is the cattle drive with McCrae, Call, and their men. Secondary is the story of the prostitute Lorena Wood, who begins in Lonesome Dove, joins the indigent former Texas Ranger Jake Spoon, and ends up traveling alongside the cattlemen, later attended somewhat inadequately by McCrae. A third involves July Johnson, a sheriff from Fort Smith, Arkansas, who is seeking to capture Jake Spoon for the accidental killing of his brother. Finally, there is the story of McCrae's former sweetheart Clara Allen, who is married to a dying man and who owns a successful horse-trading business in Ogallala, Nebraska. The story begins with McCrae and Call in Lonesome Dove, running the marginally successful Hat Creek Cattle Company, which survives by stealing already stolen stock from Mexico. McRae and other men occasionally visit Lorena, the one prostitute at the Dry Bean, a saloon owned by a French immigrant, Xavier Wance, who is hopelessly in love with Lorena. Coming home from a trip, the ex-slave Joshua Deets, one of the cattlemen and a former Ranger, returns with Jake Spoon, who was once a Ranger captain along with McCrae and Call. Spoon is a gambler and a rake, and it soon becomes clear he is undependable, a fact that is further clarified in later novels. But before he abandons his friends and Lorena, he tells them of his travels to Montana and convinces them, particularly Call, that there is a fortune to be made if they drive a herd to this as yet unsettled territory. McCrae and Call decide to follow his advice, steal a herd of cattle and horses, and begin the long journey to Montana. On the way, they encounter the West at its most pristine and most harsh, with sweeping open ranges, nearly impassable deserts, vicious outlaws, and Comancheros, including the sociopathic half-breed Blue Duck, whom McCrae and Call have encountered before as Ranger captains. In a moving sequence, McCrae meets Clara Allen again, and they confirm their love for one another and revisit the reasons why they can

never marry. In the end, after significant loses in men and resources, the Hat
Creek Cattle Company arrives in Montana and begins building a ranch. Woodrow Call, after Augustus McCrae has died, fulfills his promise to his friend by
bringing his body back to Texas and burying him in a grove of pecan trees on
the banks of the Rio Grande River near San Antonio, where McCrae had spent
time with Clara in their early years together. The story is replete with all the
conventions of epic romance. Its journey narrative, the scope and breadth of
the setting, the tale of love unrealized, are clearly mythic and archetypal. But
beneath the veneer of mythology is a set of figures that display McMurtry's capacity to create characters of depth, sympathy, contradiction, and complexity
—traits that in the course of the novel have universal as well as historical implications.

All of the novels in the saga, *Lonesome Dove* especially, are American historical romances and frontier novels, and as such they participate in a long tradition of the romance that can be traced in to the Waverley novels of Sir Walter
Scott and in America to the Leatherstocking tales of James Fenimore Cooper.
For Cooper and for other historical romancers such as William Gilmore Simms
and Robert Montgomery Bird, the setting is the American frontier, first along
the Appalachians and the Alleghenies and later, in the form of the Western, in
the Rocky Mountains and the Southwest. Central to this genre is mythogenesis,
as American writers sought to define and redefine American cultural ideology
through the figure of the frontier hero. In this context, the central thematic
tension is the conflict between the forces of historical progress and reaction. As
American civilization advances, its people seek to civilize new lands and open
new territory to settlement. But, in doing so, they transform and in many cases
eradicate an older way of life, altering and decimating the pristine lands and
taming and at times killing whole Native American tribes. The frontier hero is
both the vanguard and the victim of this process.[5] He leads expeditions into the
wilderness, assisting those who would settle these wild places. But at the same
time he has become a product of the frontier, adapted to its way of life and an
advocate for preserving the very place he helps to civilize. This is the sometimes
hidden irony in the configuration of the frontier hero and, later, the cowboy
and lawman in the Western genre. The hero represents the essential virtues of
a way of life he willingly destroys, and in the end he is himself displaced in
the process. Further, the fundamental "virtue" that defines him is violence, the
capacity to slaughter people and destroy places. It might well be argued that
the American hero in general derives from this dubious configuration and that
men such as the Founding Fathers are admired but are not America's mythic
heroes. The nation derives its concept of the heroic from the frontier figures
who violently tore a civilization from the pristine wilderness.[6]

The main characters in *Lonesome Dove* fit this pattern precisely. To the extent that they are mythic in nature, they embody all the tensions and ambiguities of the American frontiersman. Both McCrae and Call are seasoned and conditioned by the frontier experience. They have traveled west; they are alone and separated from family ties; they have learned to fight and defeat Native Americans as a part of a vanguard militia, the Texas Rangers. Finally, they have become cattle ranchers, ambivalent participants in the primary economic enterprise of the region and period. At this latter endeavor they are only marginally successful, reflecting their conflicted and intermediary status in the tension between the forces of progress and reaction. In their drive north, they are motivated yet again to find an unsettled place, to see, in their waning years, one more wilderness in its original state. But they bring with them the cattle, the men, the hammers and saws that will fell the trees and change Montana from meadow and woodland into cattle range. In the midst of this, they openly lament the loss of their way of life. Both of them have willingly forgone family in favor of the frontier. Call avoided marriage to the prostitute Maggie, whom he made pregnant with Newt Dobbs, and McCrae, with a peculiar dexterity, managed to maintain a long-term romance of the mind with Clara Allen while avoiding marriage to her, though he married two young women who died shortly after their weddings. In embracing the frontier life, they have more than implicitly endorsed its patterns of living. In fighting the Comanche and the Kiowa and defending the settlers, they have helped to bring about the demise of the old ways. Both lament deeply the passing of the frontier. As mythic characters, then, they embody all the elements and ambiguities of the frontier hero of the American historical romance, and McMurtry seems fully aware of the tensions and painful ambivalence that forms the essence of their nature.

What perhaps explains the novel in light of McMurtry's antipathy to the Western is the richness of character that has always been his hallmark. In the case of these genre-specific works, he created characters from within the pattern of myth but in doing so undermined it, particularly in McCrae and Call. Both are strong and well-adapted men of the frontier, but each has markedly different flaws and frailties. In his indolence and irresponsibility, McCrea is endearing, but these characteristics remain vices, not virtues, in the novel, perhaps somewhat in contrast to the film. As he introduces McCrae's character, McMurtry outlines his basic habits. As the rest of the troop works, he sits on the porch slowly drinking, watching the sunset, kicking pigs, and pondering: "Augustus would have mellowed for the evening and be ready for some intelligent conversation, which usually involved talking to himself. . . . As was his custom, Augustus drank a fair amount of whiskey as he sat and watched the sun ease out of the day. . . . He seldom got downright drunk, but he did enjoy feeling misty along about sundown. . . . The whiskey didn't damage his intellectual powers any, but it did make him more tolerant of the raw sorts he had to live with: Call and Pea Eye and Deets, young Newt, and old Boliver, the cook" (6–7). Unlike the typical frontier hero, Augustus is openly and unapologetically lazy, prone to visiting prostitutes, fond of card games, and, interestingly, quite introspective, an admirer of reflection and education. Despite all the time he has lived with his fellows, he is of a different sort. Ill refined though he may be, he has an almost romantic admiration for cultural refinement, and he has even carved a Latin motto he cannot read on the Hat Creek Cattle Company sign. There is an ironic tone that persists in the rendering of his character, but never so much as to challenge the basic nature presented. Unlike Call and the frontier hero myth, McCrae is thoroughly connected to the present moment, reflecting on life and ideas though lacking any concept of the future. His tendency is to respond somewhat passively to circumstances as they present themselves, and the journey to Montana is a thing he does mainly in response to Call's desires rather than his own. Clara is a partial and only a weak motive, since he is responsive more to the memory and idea of her and they will never in fact marry, even if the opportunity presents itself. Considered carefully, his lack of effort in maintaining the Hat Creek Cattle Company is inexcusable. He is a partner and times are hard, and the frontier figure would turn himself to labor without question or thought of reward. Considered practically, as identified controversially by J. Hector St. John de Crevecoeur and confirmed to a degree by later historical accounts, McCrae's behavior reflects a pattern associated with the Appalachian hill people in Tennessee from whom he is apparently descended.[7] His capacity for effort demonstrates itself only when necessary, in response to often pressing circumstances. In this context, however, the virtues of the frontier hero do appear in McCrae. He is excellent with a gun and cool under pressure, and he possesses a learned capacity to contain his fear even under the most horrific circumstances. The Native Americans he has confronted and those he meets in the course of the narrative are not conventional enemies. As he faces them, he faces more than death—he confronts unspeakable torture and indignity, a fact that, again (though inconsistent with many popular accounts of Native Americans), has been confirmed by the historical record, particularly with regard to the Comanche.[8] In spite of his apparent irresponsibility, he acts in marked contrast to Jake Spoon. McCrae is dependable under pressure and is fully capable of handling crises calmly. These are virtues that comport with the myth of the frontier hero but also exist in the actual world beyond. As such, McCrae lives beyond the myth, speaking perhaps to its only limited basis in reality.

Woodrow Call is similar to McCrae in the manner in which he embodies characteristics of the Western myth, and in some ways he is more typical of the American frontier hero than his partner and friend. He is parsimonious with words, hard working, diligent, well adapted, and knowledgeable about the practicalities of the world in which he lives. He conforms well to the mythic ideal, but he also speaks to its complexities and moral inadequacies. Early in the novel, Call is described in a combination of mythic and antimythic terms: "The funny thing about Woodrow Call was how hard he was to keep in scale. He wasn't a big man—in fact, was barely middle sized—but when you walked up and looked him in the eye it didn't seem that way. Augustus was four inches taller than his partner. . . . Augustus was the one man in south Texas who could usually keep him in scale, and he built on this advantage whenever he could. He spent many a day pitching Call a hot biscuit and remarking point-blank, 'You know, Call, you ain't really no giant' (8). This brief and humorous account of Call is in a strange sense a warning to the reader, an admonition to "keep him in scale" as the epic narrative unfolds. This proportioning is no simple task, and readers may readily respond to Call as the rest of the troop does. But McMurtry invites us to take McCrae's perspective, and the clear message is that we should recognize that Call is not all that he seems. It is reasonable to assume that as McMurtry undermines the mythic ideal, Call seeks with some struggle to reaffirm it. Call demonstrates a certain humanity insofar as he behaves the same way as anyone motivated by the frontier narrative and its character. He is a man driven by narrative, by story, and he seeks to embody what he comes to see as the most admirable traits of a culture-specific tale of heroism. But the very attempt is what humanizes him in both the best and the worse senses. McCrae is by no means a paragon of virtue, but both he and Call serve as examples of the other's inadequacy. In working his entire adult life to conform to an ideal, Call has denied himself many of the joys life offers, and he has been insensitive and unresponsive to the needs of friends and family alike. Although he is close to his men and to McCrae, through his peculiar quietude he denies them the normal regularities of friendship. He is dependable in a physical crisis but insensitive to McCrae's feelings about Clara and basically unable to enjoy much of anything but work. Further and more important, he has fathered a child, Newt Dobbs, with a prostitute, Maggie, who was hope-lessly in love with him. He abandoned Maggie and her son, taking care of the boy only after her untimely death. He never acknowledges that he is Newt's father even after taking the boy in, and though he teaches him the practicalities of life he never offers any of the more intimate gifts of patrimony. It might be argued that Call is not atypical of the nineteenth-century father, and there is certainly some truth to this. But McMurtry emphasizes Newt's need for Call's acknowledgment and the deep pain he feels in being ignored. It is interesting to note that in subsequent novels Call and Newt never come to terms, and in *Return to Lonesome Dove* the filmmakers saw fit to rectify this matter, having Call give Newt his name, thereby undermining McMurtry's darker intentions and wrapping up the narrative too cleanly. From beginning to end, Call remains a deeply problematic hero. Clara despises him, and though part of her reaction emerges from competition, she is by no means wrong. Call is in many ways emotionally dysfunctional, and his harsh indifference is never presented as a virtue. At best, it is a product of personality and circumstance, as Call's basic nature blends with the difficulties of his surroundings to create a man who is strong, dedicated to his fellows, practical, diligent, yet incapable of intimacy and more affective forms of devotion. McMurtry creates him as a peculiarly ambiguous manifestation of an ideal, a man partly of his own making and, ultimately, unmaking.

Perhaps what undermines the optative myth of the West most fully is the manner in which McMurtry embodies naturalistic themes, which are central to the novel's concept of physical reality and human nature. None of the characters, protagonists or antagonists, escape the basic impulse to engage in acts of violence. The brutality is pervasive, characterizing not only the people but the harsh landscape within which they must survive. McMurtry removes the veneer of romance that often typifies the Western and reveals the conditions that settlers often face. Violence manifests itself directly in physical acts but also in the indifference of environment and circumstance. The prostitute Lorena is brutalized by her former lover and by Jake Spoon, and she is subject to the men she must serve sexually, never acting of her own volition. Maggie is coldly abandoned by Call, and once on the cattle drive Lorena is kidnapped by Comancheros and renegade Kiowas. McMurtry is careful to render the consequences of her capture with subtlety and precision:

> Now speech had left her; fear took its place. The two white men talked constantly of killing. Blue Duck didn't talk about it, but she knew he could do it whenever it pleased him. She didn't expect to live to the end of the day—only the fact that the men weren't tired of her yet kept her alive. . . . Monkey John told her several times what he would do to her if she tried to run away—terrible things, on the order of what Blue Duck had threatened. . . . He [Monkey John] said he would sew her up with rawhide threads so tight she couldn't make water and then would watch her till she burst. (476)

McMurtry has done his research here. Accounts of brutality of this sort are common in the historical record, a reality that in the mythically constituted Western is often ignored or associated only with Native Americans.[9] *Lonesome*

Dove provides a richly ambiguous picture of the region, which is at once pure and beautiful and rapacious and violent. The line of demarcation between hero and villain, white and Native, settler and savage, is irremediably blurred. The men in this scene are metonyms for this peculiar blending. They are buffalo hunters and thieves, Native Americans, whites, and half-breeds. They clear the land of the buffalo to make way for the rancher and the settler, and they brutally rape and murder on impulse without a semblance of remorse. The West, then, is a magnet for sociopathic brutality, a place where the worst may congregate and act, and in this sense the novel broadly is an argument for the rule of law and the advancing civilization that must attend it, ironically even as murdering rapists are part of the vanguard of that advancement. The half-breed Comanchero Blue Duck is an example of this blending of the forces of progress and reaction. He is the son of Buffalo Hump, a Comanche chief drawn from history who appears in *Dead Man's Walk* and *Comanche Moon*. Blue Duck's name is taken from a nineteenth-century Cherokee outlaw who was perhaps the sometime lover of the infamous Belle Starr. Though his life and origin do not exactly parallel those of his historical counterpart, the novel's Blue Duck shares the other's penchant for senseless brutality and indifference to human suffering. He is the product of both cultures, the Comanche's and the white man's, and suggests the rapacious nature of both. At least with respect to McCrae and Call, he is a force indomitable. Again contradicting the typical Western, the narrative does not culminate in a confrontation in which heroes defeat villains. Blue Duck evades them to the end, only to be captured and executed by others who, interestingly, remain nameless.

Thus, *Lonesome Dove* is in many ways an elusive work. It is the Western that many had been encouraging McMurtry to write for years, and it reflects his deep sympathy for his region and its history. But it also demonstrates his antipathy to the Western genre in its most single-minded and mythic form. McMurtry manages a remarkable aesthetic sleight of hand in this distinctive novel, challenging and complicating the myth without rejecting it entirely. *Lonesome Dove* remains an epic romance in a conventional sense, with endearing characters that seek to find a place on the frontier, which is a realm of beauty and splendor, expansiveness and hope. But in McMurtry's vision it is by no means an open space of unambiguous possibility. As the characters traverse the Llano Estacado, the Southern Great Plains, and the Eastern Rockies into the Wyoming and Montana territories, they encounter a place indifferent to their concerns, peopled by Natives who are richly human and diverse, some kind and others brutal, often willing to defend their way of life and at times willing to acquiesce to American civilization for the most base of personal reasons. The land and its people seem always ready to kill. The land demands of those who would traverse it not only courage but fatalism: a deep sense of connectedness to place and an entrenched belief in the inevitability of even the worst of things. Characters, heroic though they may be, never seem to transcend the exigencies of time and circumstance. They fight without winning. They seek without genuinely finding. At the same time, men such as McCrae and Call remain their own immutable selves, winning in all their fallibility the sympathy of the reader and a sense of identification. The novel concludes in a moving scene as Woodrow Call returns to Lonesome Dove. He finds the burned ruins of the Dry Bean Saloon, and a reporter who has been seeking the destroyed saloon tells him that the owner burned the building around him in mourning for his lost whore, Lorena. Xavier Wance is a minor character, appearing only in the beginning and existing only in memory at the end. But his plight is shared by all who live and love. As he loses Lorena, so McCrae and Call will lose the frontier, and *Lonesome Dove* yet again embodies McMurtry's sensitivity to the forces of change as they prey upon human aspirations. In this sense, the novel is a rich rendering of a condition both universal and historical, human and deeply personal.

Streets of Laredo (1993)

Dealing with events surrounding Woodrow Call when he is approximately seventy years old, this novel concludes the *Lonesome Dove* saga, although it is only the second of four in the series. The Hat Creek Cattle Company has long since failed, and Call works independently as a bounty hunter, using the skills he learned as a Texas Ranger but dealing with the physical reality of encroaching old age. The novel offers a stark and unforgiving picture of life on a fading frontier, and Call's decline mirrors the transformation of the western region and the lifestyle he has spent his life defending. Themes of change and transience continue in this second novel, but they take a darker, more ominous turn as the one living hero of the series finds himself weakened by time and by the brutal land he has always loved.[10] The novel was ultimately adapted into a miniseries that aired in 1995 and featured an entirely different cast, with James Garner as Woodrow Call, Sissy Spacek as Lorena Wood, and Sam Shepard as Pea Eye Parker. The film also featured performances by Ned Beatty, Randy Quaid, and Wes Studi, among others. The miniseries was reviewed well, capturing many of the sentiments that greeted the first, and the extended format allowed it to faithfully render virtually all of the events of the novel. But certain cinematic choices, particularly the soundtrack, compromised the tone of the novel, which is darker and more foreboding, Lear-like in its unforgiving treatment of old age and approaching death.

McMurtry had been frustrated by the reception of *Lonesome Dove*. Having thought he had written an "anti-Western," he found that the novel was lauded as perhaps the best Western ever written. In 1991, after his bypass surgery, McMurtry lived for a time with his frequent coauthor, Diana Ossana, and while with her he experienced an bout of extreme depression, perhaps as a result of his health problems but also the result of a deep sense of self-doubt and an identity crisis that occurred with respect to his writing. It was during this time that he wrote *Streets of Laredo*. The bleak austerity of the novel perhaps reflects a combination of his personal problems and his desire to correct the popular perception of *Lonesome Dove*. What emerged was his darkest and most unrelenting confrontation with the Western myth, one that *Kirkus Reviews* called "a wonderful story" with "completely original, perfectly American characters."[11] *Streets of Laredo* garnered a number of positive reviews. In the *Los Angeles Times,* Mark Horowitz called it "one of McMurtry's most powerful and moving achievements."[12] Referring implicitly to the violence and thus the revisionist sensibility that governs the novel, Dee Brown, in the *Chicago Sun-Times,* claimed that "the dark menaces that McMurtry continually sets up—one threat succeeding another—make it impossible to set the book aside."[13] However, there was some dissent. In the *New York Times Book Review,* Noel Perrin referred to *Streets of Laredo* as a "self-parody" in comparison to *Lonesome Dove*. Acknowledging that the novel is "by no means a complete failure," he wrote that it nevertheless "makes you wish he had left the characters of *Lonesome Dove* in peace."[14] Perrin frequently referred with some frustration to the scenes of violence, which are far more numerous in this second novel in the series than in the first one, and he seemed to react negatively to the shift in tone and the bleaker, more laconic style. In comparing the novel to *Lonesome Dove,* Perrin praised the previous novel, reading it clearly as an affirmation of the Western myth. It is therefore not surprising that he reacted against the much more openly revisionist sequel.

Streets of Laredo is by McMurtry's standard a novel of average length, comprising thirty-one chapters divided into three parts and an epilogue. Continuing the pattern of *Lonesome Dove,* the book is written in the third-person omniscient, and multiple perspectives coalesce into a single narrative. The novel begins by introducing the most sympathetic characters: Woodrow Call, now an aging bounty hunter and a legend in the West; Lorena (Wood) Parker, the former prostitute who has learned to read and is now a schoolteacher; and Pea Eye Parker, the Ranger corporal, featured prominently in the previous novel, who is now Lorena's devoted husband and the father of their five children. Call is accompanied by a New York railroad agent who has hired him to capture a nineteen-year-old Mexican outlaw, Joey Garza, who has been robbing trains and brutally murdering people with a German rifle that can kill at half a mile. Call attempts to recruit Pea Eye, who first decides to stay with his family but later follows Call on his manhunt. Joey is full of hate and motivated by an uncontrollable impulse to brutality, perhaps because as a child he was been held captive by Apaches. His mother, Maria, is utterly devoted to his protection, though she knows of his horrific exploits. As the novel follows the parallel journeys of Call and Garza, two well-known Western figures appear: Judge Roy Bean (whom Joey Garza kills in the novel but who lived to a natural old age in reality) and John Wesley Hardin, the notorious outlaw and gunman. McMurtry employs these figures but clearly attempts to move beyond the folkloric softening that often attends them even in their harshest portrayals. They are brutish and violent and amoral (in the case of Judge Roy Bean more so than the historical record indicates). As the novel proceeds toward its climax, Call is severely wounded and fails to capture Joey, who murders his own mother before he is killed, ironically, by the loyal but less than heroic Pea Eye and a nameless group of townspeople. *Streets of Laredo* concludes with the crippled captain living with Pea Eye and Lorena, partially redeemed by his devotion to Maria Garza's blind daughter but haunted by a sense of failure and inadequacy. In this sense, McMurtry both criticizes and redeems the Western genre, as in *Lonesome Dove* he granted the hero a sympathy and pathos that can emerge only through a portrayal of his flaws and limitations.

In spite of his less-than-mythic status in this and other novels in the series, Call remains an admirable character who throughout this second volume retains many heroic characteristics. He is willful, courageous, industrious, and independent. As a result of his time working as a Ranger and with the cattle drive, he has become famous and highly respected. In humanizing him and undercutting the Western ideal, McMurtry is careful not to transform him into an antihero. As the novel opens, his nature, reputation, and limitations are established, and the difficult challenge he faces become clear: "Still, Brookshire had barely been able to conceal his shock when he saw how old the man was. Of course, Brookshire was aware of his reputation: no one in the West had a reputation to equal Woodrow Call's. In Brookshire's view, reputation did not catch bandits—at least it didn't catch bandits who covered the country as rapidly as young Joey Garza. The young Mexican was said to be only nineteen years old, whereas Captain Call, from the look of him, was edging seventy" (4). The carefully orchestrated contrast between the two eventual foes revolves around age, and here McMurtry makes a kind of Shakespearean move in rendering Call's limitations in human and arguably cosmological terms. He is old and he looks it, even acts it as he attempts to mount his horse. The inevitability of weakening and death are never far from the hero, making him more a figure of classical tragedy than epic. McMurtry intentionally seems to evoke these genres and the themes that naturally emerge from them. Call's greatest adversary is not Joey

Garza, and even if he were able to confront the boy and defeat him, the tragic last act of his life would remain in view. Call's greatest adversary is time, its effect upon the body and the mind, its inexorable passing, which compromises an identity it has taken Call a lifetime to build. As the narrative unfolds, so the Western myth unravels. The expected confrontation between hero and villain never occurs, perhaps upsetting readers who come to the novel expecting a conventional Western. Call is the victim of a series of unpredictable events and circumstances: the fact that Joey has a German rifle with a sight that allows him to kill from a protected distance; a chance decision when Call places himself in the range of the rifle and is shot; the fortunate arrival of Pea Eye and the Kickapoo trapper Famous Shoes, who manage to fatally wound Joey in a random interchange.

These events make Woodrow Call a player on a grand stage that reduces him but, in doing so, makes him beautifully human, even as it renders him tragic. In the end, his primary role has been to initiate the hunt. Again, though, in spite of this, Call is a man of well-earned fame, and Colonel Terry, the railroad man in the East who has sent Brookshire, has chosen well in seeking an adversary for Joey Garza. Nothing in Call's past that led to his reputation was in any way a fabrication. But Brookshire's first encounter with him clarifies the dissonance between myth and reality. Even at his best, Call was a small man who appeared larger in his actions and demeanor. Myth and reality are co-implicated but different, and Call's reputation, elevated to mythic levels, takes him beyond history into a realm of half-truth, the misty yet colorful realm of folklore. His past serves to exaggerate his sense of failure in the end. Joey Garza has been killed, but Call cannot and will not take credit, and his growing sense of weakness and his loss of his leg and arm, as well as his deep sense of inadequacy, plague him. The only redemption he experiences is in his devotion to the blind sister of Joey Garza, whom Call cares for and will ultimately perhaps send away to school. His ultimate status is neither heroic nor antiheroic. It is real, tragic in a certain way but, as such, full of pathos that evokes our sympathy.

McMurtry's transformation of the frontier hero speaks to his use of the American historical romance as genre. In challenging the contours of the form in *Streets of Laredo* and altering the basic characteristics of its central character, McMurtry amplifies the literary naturalism introduced in *Lonesome Dove*. Literary naturalism as it emerged in the 1890s was never divorced from the romance tradition, and in its treatment of violence *Streets of Laredo* makes powerful use of elements of the gothic and grotesque. As in the gothic genre at its best, events are presented realistically, along with the interior psychology of characters that are perverse or in distress. But the gothic involves a conscious heightening of the horrific that other genres soften and keep from view. In *Streets of Laredo,* McMurtry understands the nineteenth-century West as a place where brutality, violence, and criminally psychopathic behavior often reigned. This becomes clear in the character of Joey Garza, who is a monster who kills without remorse. But it is even more obvious in the man-burner Mox Mox, a pyromaniac mass murderer who takes brutality to another level entirely: "Mox Mox had probably killed the old Comanche woman because she was short. She was about the same height as Mox Mox himself. Burning flesh smelled sweet—that was a fact soon learned, if you rode with Mox Mox. . . . Mox Mox wasn't paying much attention to this fire, or to the old woman's burning. Most likely, that was because she was dead, and couldn't scream and plead. When people screamed and pleaded, Mox Mox got icy cool. He was like the sleet at such times" (251). In presenting certain verifiable circumstances through an unflinching and vivid portrayal, McMurtry calls attention to the necessity of resistance, affirming at least the need for individuals who in some way manifest the characteristics of the frontier hero. This accounts certainly for Call's ambiguous status as the mythic man of the West. From a political standpoint, though McMurtry questions the myths that affirmed the Westward expansionist project, he calls attention to the need for civilization and the rule of law, since without those rules people like Joey and Mox Mox would run free, murdering and plundering at will. Without the structures of civilization, the West becomes a magnet for rapacious madness. But, in another sense, particularly from a naturalist perspective, there is nothing that can combat the indifferent processes of nature that these villains in part represent. At times, those processes seem arbitrary, at other times actively malevolent. But, in the harsh landscape of McMurtry's West, human beings are subject to natural and mysterious forces that circumscribe their fate, and there is little that men like Call can do to alter the inevitability of destruction. Heroism lies, then, not in victory but in stoic resistance to violence and in a measured respect for nature and time.

In this sense, McMurtry employs some of the darkest themes in American literature, reflecting that strand in the tradition of the American novel that emphasizes a darker, more deterministic worldview. But there is a lighter, more redemptive counterpoint to this seeming hopelessness. It is the comfort of home, human commitment, and family. In *Lonesome Dove,* Pea Eye Parker is a confirmed bachelor, the last man one would expect to end up married to Lorena and far from a romantic figure. In that sense, her choice of him is unlikely. But Pea Eye in most ways has been an entirely sympathetic if quiet character. He was a loyal corporal in the company and a devoted friend, especially to

Joshua Deets, and he withstood with courage the attack by Natives that eventually killed McCrae. All of these traits he brings forward, and, outside the action of the novel, he emerges as Lorena's man of choice, in contrast even to the younger Dish Boggett. In a strange sense, family and home are the novel's angle of repose. The story begins and ends in the sanctuary shared by Pea Eye and Lorena. This is certainly affirmed in the conflict Pea Eye experiences when he initially decides not to accompany Call. Pea Eye's eventual desire to follow Call is motivated not by the fact that his loyalty to the captain is greater, but because Call, with his age and weakness, displays the greatest need. As Lorena follows, she breaks many of the gender boundaries typical of the Western by facing the threat of Mox Mox and traveling with Call through the harsh landscape of Texas and Mexico despite his protestations. This heroism, displayed by both Pea Eye and Lorena, is demonstrated in service of the primary ethic of loyalty—not to a cause but to friends and family.

This same commitment is displayed by Maria Garza in her admirable and unflinching commitment to her son Joey. She has lived and tried to raise her children under the most degrading of circumstances. She is a woman in Mexico. She has been married three times, and one of her indigent husbands sold Joey to the Apaches. After Joey's return and his transformation into a brutal thief and murderer, her commitment to him remains steadfast, and she is devoted to protecting him from anyone who would harm him. She is caught between Joey and her other two children, whom Joey frequently abuses, but she refuses to choose against him, even as she tries to protect her blind daughter and her mentally challenged son against Joey and other threats. She is a woman of utter commitment and consummate maternal virtue, sacrificing all other ethical considerations for her family. In the end, she makes the ultimate sacrifice. In his unwarranted hatred for Maria, the wounded and dying Joey, in a fit of rage, fatally wounds his mother with a knife. Even then, Maria remains loyal; as she lies in bed, dying, she caresses the son who murdered her. The novel's darkness is never compromised, but it is counterbalanced, as in other naturalistically oriented works, by the vivid picture of maternalistic commitment and brotherhood.

Thus, in *Streets of Laredo* McMurtry attempts to set the record straight, heightening and emphasizing themes and circumstances he had introduced in *Lonesome Dove*. In the previous novel, characters were heroic but far from triumphant, and villainy and naturalistic brutality appeared ubiquitous. But in the sequel, McMurtry seems acutely aware of the pervasive appeal of the Western and the tendency in audiences to ignore certain details of plot and changes in convention that tend to undermine the heroic status of the central characters. In *Streets of Laredo,* McMurtry abandons all subtlety. The story of Call in old age could have remained untold. Or Call could have risen above his existential circumstances. He could have defeated Joey Garza and recovered from his wounds. Pea Eye could have remained the loyal second man instead of the unwitting killer of the novel's primary villain. Lorena could have followed the pattern of women in other Westerns and been passive and obedient, weak and dependent. But McMurtry is direct and unflinching in his portrayal of a darker concept of the Western and its characters. Circumstance reigns, and people must negotiate their way through a world that reduces them. In all of this, *Streets of Laredo,* if an "anti-Western," is nuanced and ambiguous. The brutality and malevolence of Joey Garza and Mox Mox are defeated. The more sympathetic characters live on. Call retains enough of his former strength to kill the man-burner, and he withstands the pain and indignity of permanent injury. McCrae chose to die rather than live a crippled man; Call (though never presented with the option) never genuinely considers this possibility, and readers are left to decide who is more heroic, which character is more consistent with the general concept of the frontier hero. In spite of all of the novel's stark revisionism, it remains in one important way a genuine Western in the best sense of the tradition. It is a striking evocation of the land, in all its harsh beauty and limitless scope. In *Streets of Laredo,* the West of McMurtry's "reality" remains in many ways the West of the American imagination.

Dead Man's Walk (1995)

Dead Man's Walk, the third novel in the saga but a prequel to *Lonesome Dove,* takes readers back to the time when Augustus McCrae and Woodrow Call meet as Texas Rangers in their early twenties. Obviously, the narrative marks an inception, as it recounts the growth and coming age of the heroes. But it also introduces (even in comparison to *Streets of Laredo*) McMurtry's darkest, most historically grounded, and most vividly honest portrayal of the American West. The Natives are unspeakably brutal; the white leaders are incompetent and corrupt; the Rangers are often confused and powerless; and the landscape is beautiful and harsh beyond imagining. In this context, McCrae and Call appear at their youngest and most vulnerable. It is clear in this novel especially that McMurtry has done his research, and in continuing his attempt to create a saga of "anti-Westerns" he is unwilling to adopt common and sometimes romantic conceptions of settlers, adventurers, Native Americans, and the land itself. It is in the midst of human degradation and depravity that the young heroes must enter manhood, and neither of them is endowed with the benefits of a positive upbringing. They emerge from the mists of the past, with few details about their childhood provided, each with demons that do not always present themselves as obvious but that nevertheless affect them as they embark on a problematic process of self-understanding and identity formation.

Dead Man's Walk is a relatively brief novel of four parts with a total of fifty-seven chapters, and like the previous two novels in the saga it is written from the third-person omniscient point of view. Critics seemed to understand McMurtry's desire to emphasize his dark antimythic perception of the West and his intention to explore the problematic development of gender-specific codes of behavior. In the *New York Times Book Review*, Thomas Flanagan saw *Lonesome Dove* and *Dead Man's Walk* as "freestanding yet linked . . . carrying forward to their ultimate limit the themes and leather tough atmospherics on which novels and films of the Texas frontier depend."[15] The texture of the novel is vividly accurate, and the historical events recounted are largely so, portraying the exploits of Texas Rangers in 1840 as they encountered and attempted to defeat the Comanche, Kiowa, and Apache in the Republic of Texas. The novel begins as the young Ranger troop is led by the doomed and hapless leader Major Randall Chevallie into the Comancheria, where they encounter the indomitable Comanche chief Buffalo Hump. After some losses, including that of Chevallie, the Rangers find their way back to Austin, but not before a darkly comic sequence in which McCrae takes a spear in the buttocks driven by the brutal chief, who later vows to kill him for escaping death from his lance. Once in town, McCrae meets and courts Clara Forsythe, the Clara Allen of *Lonesome Dove*, and Call spends his spare time with the luckless Maggie Tilton, the prostitute who will give birth to his son Newt. After a time, McCrae and Call join the historical Santa Fe Expedition, which was intended to enable the annexation of a portion of Mexico east of the Rio Grande. In their journey, they must contend with hostile Natives of different tribes, the elements of nature, and physical and emotional starvation. In addition, they must deal with the rash and incompetent leadership of Caleb Cobb, who is an ex-pirate and a fortune hunter, courageous but inexperienced and selfish and unconcerned with the lives of others. They begin with nearly two hundred men and, at the end of the failed exhibition, return with forty. In the meantime, they are routed by Comanche and captured by the very Mexicans they intended to defeat. They are then forced to march the treacherous Jornada del Muerto, or Dead Man's Walk, which takes them two hundred miles to El Paso to face the Mexican authorities. Here McMurtry takes some historical liberties. In reality, the scene in which the men are required to draw a bean from a jar to determine whether they will be executed is drawn from the Mier Expedition of 1842. The historical Bigfoot Wallace, executed in the bean exchange in *Dead Man's Walk*, was present during the Mier event but lived until 1899. The young Rangers, after surviving, agree to escort an English gentlewoman cursed with leprosy to Austin. She is mannered, confident, genteel, and strange, and the novel reaches its climax as she rides naked toward a group of Comanche led by Buffalo Hump, singing an aria with a boa constrictor around her neck. The novel introduces a host of colorful characters: the two-hundred-pound prostitute Matilda Roberts and the adventurers Bigfoot Wallace and Shadrach. There is even an encounter with the rancher Charlie Goodnight in his youth, though in reality at this time he would have been a young boy. The novel, then, dramatizes the process by which McCrae and Call learn their skills as Texas Rangers, make their initial choices as to lifestyle and vocation, and learn their limitations as they confront the harshness of the American West in a time before settlement has taken hold.

In terms of genre, *Dead Man's Walk* is a bildungsroman or "coming of age" novel, one that participates in the tradition of the American historical romance and contains elements of the gothic and the carnivalesque. Equally focused on McCrae and Call, the narrative enters both characters' minds as they cope with extraordinary circumstances and an unforgiving and frequently brutal world. Unlike the main characters in many heroic narratives, these young men are not on a path to genuine self-sufficiency and triumphal agency.

They are distinctly modern heroes, as they learn to live in a largely deterministic universe, one that seems barely aware of their existence much less their individual concerns, hopes, and sufferings. This is the lesson they must learn as frontier mythic figures in the making, a lesson different from the one readers might expect the hero in a typical Western to confront. In the more common generic novels, the young frontiersman gains control of himself and his world through a violence that is justified by an ideologically grounded set of virtues. McCrae and Call come to be motivated by a more humble goal—simply to stay alive, to avoid ignominious death as long as they can. In this objective, they must come to terms with the external threats of nature and the Natives, but they must also deal with the internal forces of trepidation and panic that their daily experiences evoke. We see this struggle on the first journey in the novel, that of Augustus McCrae. He and Call have been assigned a night watch, and in his impatience McCrae decides to go for a walk, to go "prospecting," as he calls it. In the midst of a lightning storm he encounters the real but, under the circumstances, ghostly image of Buffalo Hump. This event reveals much more than the Comanche chief's strength and skill. It illuminates the interior conflict of an emerging but problematic Western figure in McCrae: "He had meant to wait—it was sensible to wait, and yet a feeling had come over him that told him to move. The feeling told him to run. . . . As he trotted, Gus began to realize that he was scared. The feeling that came over him, that brought him to his feet and started him trotting, was fear . . . he was driven to trot through the darkness by an overpowering sense that *somebody* was near" (44). Perhaps the most striking thing about this passage is the manner in which McCrae is simultaneously humanized and animalized. In sensing something and experiencing the onset of fear, he has feelings that are immediately recognizable and commonly shared. At the same time, however, McCrae is motivated by the kind of animal instinct to flee that can be found in characters in the naturalist novels of writers such as Stephen Crane, Jack London, Theodore Dreiser, and Frank Norris. McCrae's response most vividly recalls that of Henry Fleming in Crane's *The Red Badge of Courage,* in which the impulse to run comes immediately and without warning and the act of fleeing occurs seemingly without volition. It is only in the midst of involuntary action that the rational human mind powerlessly ponders the instinctual actions of the body. Augustus McCrae becomes an animal in flight, driven by a peculiar but observable foresight or instinctual sense. But, in the process, he also emerges as distinctly human in his rational capacity to name his emotion, to categorize it and comprehend its distinctive nature. He can mark out his fear from others' feelings and ultimately identify its source, and in the process he comes to consciously understand the internal struggle he must engage in if he is to survive on the frontier. In the face of the Comanche, a storied tribe of warriors who delight not only in killing but also in torturing their captives in the most horrific ways, McCrae must maintain his composure, focus his physical and mental energies, learn not to panic, and finally understand that his survival is as dependent on chance as it is upon any action he might take.

For McMurtry, this is the lesson of the frontier West, and it must be learned equally by Call, who responds to these circumstances both in similar and in different ways. As McCrae simply confronts his fears and understands that they must be understood and contained, Call responds by actively learning the practices of the frontiersman. He is by no means deluded into thinking that competence offers any guarantees of survival and safety. He simply accepts that in understanding the practicalities and defenses, the learned practices of the Rangers, he materially increases the possibility that he will survive. Even so, his silent and stoic approach to work becomes a kind of ritual, a means of ordering the uncertainly and mystery of his world. This kind of ritual practice is a coping mechanism explored by other twentieth-century writers, particularly by Ernest Hemingway in "The Big Two-Hearted River." In this two-part short story, Nick Adams has returned from war and is on a solitary fishing trip in the Michigan woods. There he gains a sense of calm by observing specific methods of fishing and making camp. He elevates them to rituals as order and competence in work serve to moderate the effects of his traumatic experience. Call employs work and pursues and understanding of frontier methods for precisely the same reasons. As frontier figures in the making, McCrae and Call gain control over nothing but themselves, as nature and circumstance remain indomitable forces in their lives and ultimately hold sway.

Nature itself is the primary obstacle with which they must contend. But, under most circumstances, with proper preparation, they can deal with its challenges. The truly unpredictable and infinitely more frightening force is the Natives, specifically the Comanche and the Apache, in the figures of Buffalo Hump and the Apache horse thief Kicking Wolf. In his effort to represent them accurately, McMurtry is forthright, courageous, and unflinching. Contemporary treatments of Native Americans, though positive and responsive to the realities of historical injustice and territorial displacement, are often simplistic and rife with generalizations, often painting very different tribes with a broad romantic brush. In a thoroughly researched and detailed history of Qaunah Parker and his mother, Cynthia Ann Parker, S. C. Gwynne provided a more nuanced portrait that humanizes and renders complex both Natives and whites. Regarding acts of torture and cruelty in warfare, he wrote:

> . . . some chroniclers ignore the brutal side of Indian life altogether. . . . But certain facts are inescapable: American Indians were warlike by nature, and they were warlike for centuries before Columbus stumbled upon them. . . . Most important, the Indians themselves saw absolutely nothing wrong with these acts. For westering settlers, the great majority of whom believed in the idea of absolute good and evil, and thus universal standards of moral behavior, this was nearly impossible to understand. . . . Comanches had no dominant, unified religion, or anything like a single God . . . there was no ultimate good or evil: just actions and their consequences. (44–45)

Across the continent from the beginning, there was a plethora of Native tribes as diverse in their values and cultural practices as any people in the world at large. What they shared was preindustrial modes of economy; some were settled agrarians and some, nomadic hunter gatherers. In their encounters with white Europeans, these tribes quickly adapted many European tools and mechanisms for survival to their own way of life, and in some cases they possessed value systems foreign and abhorrent to a modern, post-Enlightenment sensibility. They were by no means "savage" in the sense that they were precultural. But the best archeological accounts suggest that some tribes were peaceful and some violent; for the ancient Pueblo peoples, the commitment to peace was so strong that it appears to have enabled subsequent tribes to displace them. The Comanche, other Southwestern tribes such as the Apache and the Kiowa, and the peoples of the northern plains quickly emerged as new and distinct cultural entities after the Spanish introduced the horse to the North American continent. Elements of the tribes' oral traditions preceded them in previous cultural configurations in the region. But these oral tales were radically changed over time as new circumstances presented a need for new mythologies. The Comanche quickly became expert horsemen and built a culture around the two practices of buffalo hunting and raiding. Theirs was a warrior society built on rigid patriarchal models and a fundamental ethic of violence. McMurtry captures these historical facts in vivid narrative detail, while at the same time rendering the Natives heroic. Buffalo Hump is drawn from history, though the events describing him in *Dead Man's Walk* are largely fictional. What distinguishes him from the hapless Rangers on both journeys is (in precise naturalist terms) the fact that he is thoroughly adapted to the land he occupies. Much of what might be called deplorable in Buffalo Hump's character—his viciousness, brutality, and torturous avarice—is mirrored in the harsh landscape he occupies. As that landscape is indifferent to suffering, so is Buffalo Hump. As it is brutal and unforgiving, so is the indomitable chief. The Rangers can only hope for incidents of luck and happenstance. For a time anyway, he is simply stronger than they. Interestingly, they escape from him in their final journey because of Lady Carey, who introduces an element of unpredictability as she rides naked with her head cloaked and singing a European aria, thus introducing a foreign and unrecognizable threat to the environment and giving the Natives pause. In this sense, McMurtry deals with the Native Americans and whites in the best naturalist fashion, as environment conspires with circumstance to produce a result devoid of traditional heroism. McMurtry's Natives are the Native Americans of history: forceful, heroic, adaptable, violent, and victimized.

All of this takes place in the context of a western landscape rendered with McMurtry's distinctive vision, narrative style, and laconic voice, and the land itself retains an element of mythic association while enriching and challenging the flat romantic contours of the Western myth. The largeness of the land—its aridity, lifelessness, and otherworldly quality—only heightens the characters' sense of its harsh indifference. McMurtry rarely describes the landscape alone; usually the land appears in relation to and in confrontation with people. As an emblem of America itself, McMurtry's western spaces, and the people that traverse them in *Dead Man's Walk*, mirror the nation itself in the 1840s. Expansionist ambitions find expression at roughly the same time, interestingly, in John O'Sullivan's concept of Manifest Destiny. In this historical context, McMurtry is careful to render the landscape vividly: "They watched closely as the Comanche raiders rode down into the shallow valley—just a cleft between two ridges, really. In the distance, they could see a curve of the Rio Rojo. The wind was blowing hard from the north; spumes of sand curled over the lip of the ridge to the north and blew into the eyes of the Mexican captives" (455).

Unlike many Western writers, McMurtry chooses not to treat landscape discretely here. The novel is always about the confrontation between the land and the people who are attempting, vainly, to conquer or subdue it. There is an ambiguity drawn from reality in this particular rendering. The place is rough, with clefts and ridges, and harsh as the wind sends "spumes" of dust into the faces of those who, perhaps mistakenly, have the audacity to confront the full force of a land that reduces them. It is a landscape that works in intimate relation with the interiors of character as it becomes the outer reflection of their own desolation. In the midst of their fears and grasping hope of survival, McCrae and Call find that the land is always there, tiring them, breaking them down, and in the end sustaining them. Nature acts as a kind of harsh father, initiating them into manhood, and it is from these western lands that the Comanche and the Apache emerge, never separate from but always a part of the terrain, fully integrated, as if one could not exist without the other. The vision presented seems bereft of political ideology; the land is neither pristine nor wasted. It is not presented as a thing to be preserved, and in no way can it be conquered or exploited, at least not under the circumstances of the novel. It simply exists as a thing that must be understood and accepted.

In this rigidly naturalist context, in the end McMurtry introduces an element of the carnivalesque and grotesque, romantic motifs that have frequently been employed by writers of a naturalist sensibility. The young Rangers have agreed to escort Lady Carey to Austin, but in a peculiar twist of irony she becomes their escort and protector. She is a leper, and they never see her face. But her condition is made more evocative and disturbing by her strength, courage, and genteel manner. In the tradition of the romantic grotesque, she makes of herself a genuine work of art, cloaking herself in finery and traveling with pride and dignity. Echoing the carnivalesque, she uses the very strangeness of her appearance to save them. Riding naked on a horse, her scars and blemishes in full view, she confronts the Comanche: "Lady Carey, on a fine black gelding, started up the long ridge toward the Comanche, the boa draped over her shoulders. She was still singing her scales, but before she had gone more than a few feet she stopped the scales and began to sing, high and loud, in the Italian tongue. . . . She felt in good voice. The aria she was singing came from Signor Verdi's new opera *Nabucco*—he had taught her the aria himself, two years ago in Milan, not long before she and her husband, Lord Carey, sailed together for Mexico" (469). Of course, the grotesque peculiarity of the scene saves the travelers from a massacre, precisely because she does not comport with any world the Comanche know and are adapted to. But the strangeness that surrounds her, orchestrated in the form of the literary grotesque in juxtaposition with discordant qualities—beauty and decay together with the shocking sound of the aria in the midst of the desert—is as unsettling for the lead characters as it is for their adversaries. In the most striking scene involving a confrontation with the land, McMurtry, through these romantic motifs, introduces an element of mystery and the sublime. In a novel centered on the initiation of two problematic young heroes into a problematic manhood, it is this very strangeness and mystery—of the western land and its people—that informs their experience from beginning to end.

Comanche Moon (1997)

This fourth novel in the saga and the third in the sequence of events, *Comanche Moon* is a story that cannot easily be told. The novel presents McCrae and Call in their prime, at the height of their powers, when they become captains in the Texas Rangers and fight the Comanche. In a series of novels that are designed explicitly to undermine and scrutinize the Western myth, *Lonesome Dove* has made this final novel a difficult story to render. In *Lonesome Dove*, it is understood that McCrae and Call have earned genuine respect and renown and are remembered for their heroic exploits in service of the settlers and the state of Texas. This presents a problem for an author attempting to create characters who are not overtly heroic. But this very problem leads to a particularly nuanced representation of the Western archetype. The two heroes genuinely deserve the designation. They are courageous, tenacious, skilled in warfare, at times even indomitable in spirit. Further, following the pattern of the frontier hero, they are wanderers, avoiding long-term marriage and settled commitment. Most important, they are irremediably violent. But McMurtry remains conscious of the setting and the context he has created in previous novels, and in representing these characters at their height he is willing to disappoint anyone who expects a dramatic apotheosis of the Western mythic story. McCrae and Call, even at their best, are the unwitting victims and beneficiaries of circumstance. The world they face is too formidable for any individual to confront alone, and though they approach it with resolve, they are caught yet again in a deterministic realm of chance and indifference. Their survival has something to do with their developed qualities as heroes, but even with those characteristics they remain alive in large part through a random confluence of events that conspire in their favor. In this sense, the Western myth is affirmed only insofar as it is reconfigured. McCrae and Call lack the kind of conscious agency typical of traditional heroes, and for all their appeal they become ethically problematic tools in a process of westward expansion that will transform the land irremediably and forever.

Reviews of *Comanche Moon* were few in number and at best mixed. In many ways it was impossible to capture the reality that had led to the aura of past heroism that clung to the main characters in *Lonesome Dove.* McMurtry's refusal to elevate their status seemed to frustrate some critics, many of whom hoped for the ultimate apotheosis of the Western apparently promised in the first novel in the series. However, writing for the *New York Times Book Review,* Andy Solomon, perhaps because he was a literary scholar schooled in the Western in its various configurations, seemed to grasp McMurtry's purpose. He wrote:

> In *Comanche Moon,* McMurtry has created a sprawling, picaresque novel that, like the history of the West itself, leaves more than a few loose ends. Some characters' fates we can only surmise. Others await resolution in *Lonesome Dove.* As usual, characters are the novel's strength. McMurtry's rangers are heroic because of their vulnerabilities, not despite them. . . . His Comanche are respected, not romanticized. When Buffalo Hump rides off to die, he is grateful for "the knowledge that in the years of his youth and manhood he had drawn the lifeblood of so many enemies." . . . In the heroic time of *Comanche Moon,* these men [McCrae and Call] set out to tame the West; just a few years later. . . they will finally be tamed themselves.[16]

It is character and the spirit of history that give the novel its strength. McMurtry manages in the series in general to create in McCrae and Call characters that will appeal to those drawn to the Western myth and perhaps adhere to its implicit nationalistic and expansionist ideology. But in *Comanche Moon,* McMurtry must lay down all his chips, and again the characters, while retaining their merits as heroes to a degree, are caught in the inexorable sweep of a history they do not control and have not consciously orchestrated.

Solomon is correct in calling the novel a sprawling, picaresque work. *Comanche Moon* is an expansive novel of three parts, totaling 135 chapters. It is picaresque in terms of the loose and episodic nature of the narrative. The plot takes the characters on a series of adventures that reveal their nature and conflicts, but McMurtry seems unwilling to organize these events around any overarching structural motif such as the journey. Rather, the novel fictionalizes (at times quite thinly and with many liberties taken) a series of random and chaotic events centered on the settlement of Texas and the wars with the various Comanche tribes. Book One focuses on the torture and captivity of Inish Scull, the captain who elevates McCrae and Call to Ranger captains so that he can travel on foot to recapture his stolen horse. Scull is a bit of a comic figure—Harvard educated, highly mannered, full of high sentence—but, unlike the captains in *Dead Man's Walk,* he is genuinely heroic. He is taken by a well-known and brutal bandit, Ahumado, who hangs Scull over a cliff in a cave and later in a pit, giving him just enough food and water to survive as he slowly goes mad. After returning for a time to Austin, McCrae and Call spend time with Clara Forsyth and Maggie Tilton. McCrae is deeply in love with Clara, who ardently returns his affections. But he is also a wanderer and she knows it, and the pragmatist in her accepts the attentions of the more stable Bob Allen. Call spends time with the sympathetic but hapless prostitute Maggie, who has given birth to his child, Newt. He is helpful but unwilling to commit, and their relationship ends with her untimely death from disease.

Book Two deals with the rescue of Scull by McCrae and Call, the adulterous exploits of Scull's wife, Inez, the accidental and unceremonious death of Ahumado from a spider bite and a fall from a cliff, and the continued relationships of the Rangers and the ladies. It culminates with a fictional rendering of the Great Raid of 1840 (though in the novel it takes place in 1860), in which Buffalo Hump, having united various Comanche bands, sweeps across the Texas Plains in a desperate effort to avoid the reservation. Book Three is set seven years later, after the close of the Civil War. Scull has fought heroically for the Union and is elevated to the rank of general. McCrae and Call have remained Texas Rangers, fighting the Comanche. Clara has married Bob Allen, and McCrae mourns the death of Nellie, his second wife, this loss coming after only one year of marriage. Call ultimately breaks all ties to Maggie, who soon dies, and the novel ends (if it can be called an ending) with another fictionalization of actual history. The Texas Rangers raid the camp of the Comanche chief Peta Nocona and rescue his wife, Cynthia Anne Parker, a captive who has been fully acclimated into the Comanche tribe and has given birth to its last great leader, Quanah Parker. Again, McMurtry returns to his original source for the characters, as Charles Goodnight, the loose prototype for Woodrow Call, was actually in attendance at the raid. The novel is full of events, texture, and character but thin in terms of structure, refusing to satisfy readers' desire to see its heroes portrayed in a fully triumphant light.

Among the features that distinguish McCrae and Call from other Western heroes are their rich interiority and reflectiveness. In Book Three, after McCrae has lost Nellie, he becomes uncharacteristically remote. Normally a man inclined to social interaction, he leaves Austin and travels west of town for days, and when the governor wants to send him on another expedition, two of his men, Pea Eye Parker and the Kickapoo tracker Famous Shoes, have to find him. McCrae has left to ponder deep things, which he can do only in solitude. As he encounters his men, he reveals what appears to be only an inkling of his thoughts:

> "I'm glad you ain't dead, Captain," Pea Eye said. "I'm real glad you ain't dead."

"No, I ain't dead," Augustus told him. "I just rode off to think for a few days, and one of the things I wanted to think about was the fact that I ain't dead."

"Why would you need to think about that, Captain?" Pea asked.

"Well, because people die," Augustus said. "Two of my wives are dead. Long Bill Coleman is dead. Quite a few of the men I've rangered with are dead—three of them died right on this hill we're standing on." (616)

The question McCrae leaves to ponder is a telling one given his ambiguous status as hero. Western frontier figures confront death continually, and of course they approach it with a degree of stoicism. But they also possess a high degree of agency. The reason they are alive and others are not is their bravery and skill, the inner fortitude they embody, all a part of their status as mythic heroes of the frontier. It is these human qualities that ultimately imply that human beings through force of will have power over circumstances and the land, and only in rare situations does chance intervene and decide their fate. As he ponders the fact that he remains alive, McCrae takes no credit, implying that his survival in the face of violence and disease is rather a mystery, explainable only through a sense that he is subject to forces beyond himself that he cannot understand. As a hero, he is simultaneously elevated and reduced by this quiet realization. He is elevated in a sense that he confronts a reality more frightening than the Comanche he has fought, a metaphysical dread and an existential crisis that can be battled to a draw only by inner fortitude. He is reduced by his lack of free will and has little control over his ultimate fate, as death selects whom it chooses with horrifying unpredictability. McCrae casually picks up some arrowheads and jokes with his men, saying that perhaps they will bring him luck. In a telling moment of prophecy, Famous Shoes says, "You already have luck" (617). McCrae survives not because of his traditional heroic virtues but because of the mysterious good fortune that has always attended him, a luck that will ultimately take its leave.

These intense naturalistic themes are balanced by a sense of comic absurdity, revealed primarily in the characters of Inish and Inez Scull. The black humor that defines their characters by no means contradicts the notion of dark determinism that attends McCrae and Call. Instead, McMurtry's use of the comic mode serves to heighten these themes through a generic contrast. Inish Scull and his wife, dysfunctional though they may be as a couple, are in a sense perfect for each other. Both are fiercely independent but ill equipped for the regularities of common life. McCrae and Call are elevated to captain initially only because Scull decides to venture into hostile territory to recover a stolen horse. Though academic in inclination and manner, he has decided to make history rather than teach it, and as he brazenly heads toward Ahumado's camp he shows no sign of fear, instead displaying a stubborn and humorous sense of personal invulnerability.

Even after he is captured, he remains resilient and defiant, and his actions make Ahumado almost curious. As he hangs in the cage singing and attracting birds, Ahumado muses that he is good at catching them. Later, placed in a pit to slowly die, he sings and recites, ignoring the snakes and other torments that attend him. Even as he goes mad, his defiance remains, a defiance that oddly defeats Ahumado, not through confrontation but through stubborn resolve. His circumstance seems in many ways a grand metaphor for a universal existential condition, Beckett-like as its character in comic madness confronts the hopeless absurdity of his circumstances. In Scull's case, this embrace of the ridiculous leads to his survival and dubious triumph, as he goes on to become a hero in the American Civil War. He is eccentric and strange, victorious and heroic but unromantic, the perfect match for his promiscuous wife. Inez Scull defies all expectations, and through her McMurtry takes aim at one of the most cherished American cultural patterns—the myth of Southern womanhood. Inez is in many ways the quintessential Southern aristocratic woman. She is rich, and she embraces that status aggressively but comfortably. She buys out the general store with a sense of entitlement that one could expect only from someone raised as an aristocrat. She is materialistic, entitled, and dependent. But her character becomes another absurd rendering of type. As Inish Scull becomes a parody of a nineteenth-century gentleman of honor and marshal virtue, so Inez Scull becomes a parody of the Southern belle. Unrestrained and with the full knowledge (though not consent) of her husband, she pursues sex with a comic abandon, sleeping with men until she is tired of them and then moving on. She begins with Jake Spoon and continues with Augustus McCrae, and after Scull's return from the war she even makes it impossible for them to retain a butler, driving one away because of her (in Inish Scull's academic term) persistent attempts to "copulate" with him. She manifests all the traits of Southern womanhood in her aristocratic bearing and values, but she defies that image directly by rejecting the ideal of purity commonly associated with the myth. Her husband helps to undermine the ideal through his frustrated acceptance of her exploits and vices, coupled with a seeming lack of concern about them. Again, through both characters, Inish and Inez Scull, McMurtry takes aim at another set of American myths, dismantling them as he encourages the readers to feel some quiet joy at their late demise.

In many ways, *Comanche Moon* requires a sophisticated critical sensibility to be appreciated, and to understand the novel one certainly must be aware of McMurtry's attitude toward the Western genre, whether that awareness comes from a careful reading of the previous books or from McMurtry's public statements on the matter. Read in this context, however, *Comanche Moon* emerges as a tremendously well-wrought culmination of the *Lonesome Dove* saga. Its heroes are admirable but flawed, limited in agency but endearing in their humanity. Other characters complement them in either their comic nature or their quiet resemblance not to figures often configured as type but to genuine people whose fears and hopes are recognizable in any epoch. In this sense, in dismantling the Western genre McMurtry succeeds in the much more difficult task of reconfiguring it for the modern and postmodern age. The Western remains the American morality play, the genre though which the nation seeks to discover, consider, and reconsider its identity, always in sympathetic terms, and in a richly human sphere of action and understanding.

CHAPTER 6

Other Works

In a vast collection of writings and reflections in many genres—from fiction, to essays, to film and television scripts—Larry McMurtry has dealt with themes of quest, hope, desire, sexuality, youth, and old age, all in a richly human and culturally textured context. His greatest strength is certainly characterization, which has consistently led him to the novel as a means of expression. He has managed to work within the context of a number of subgenres, and certainly in the case of the novel of manners he transforms it in substantive ways, mainly through a studied disregard of tightly structured plot in favor of incidents that mirror his character's experience. But his works are full of situations in which people struggle with various historically grounded concerns. At the heart of his work is a preoccupation with modernity—the process by which it emerged, its various social manifestations in cities and on the land, its shaping effects on the identities of thinking individuals only partially and painfully aware of the complex forces that circumscribe their daily lives. McMurtry has returned to these preoccupations with a continuous force and determination in novel after novel, in film after film, and, notably, in a number of essay collections that address social and historical concerns directly. Many of his less considered works, those that have received scant attention from scholars, nevertheless illuminate these interests and enrich our understanding of his body of work as a whole.

Anything for Billy (1988)

During the years he was writing the *Lonesome Dove* saga, McMurtry took time to create another tale of the American West. *Anything for Billy* is a lighthearted satire of the Western myth, taking Billy the Kid as its central subject. It is a novel of average length, comprising six parts, told from the point of view of a lovable and strangely antiheroic dime novelist, Ben Sippy. The narrator encounters Billy (in the novel referred to as Billy Bone) and his partner, Joe Lovelady, somewhat randomly on the New Mexico plains. The two men take him in and absorb him in a series of adventures that are largely McMurtry's fictional creation. The historical Lincoln County Wars become the Whisky Glass War, and the major characters change, having been replaced by a host of colorful Western antitypes that form the substance of a playfully ironic tale. Ben Sippy is a wealthy urbanite from Philadelphia who (out of boredom with his wife and nine daughters) becomes obsessed with reading dime novels about the American West, so obsessed that he begins writing them and ultimately emerges as one of the world's most popular writers of cheap Western yarns. After a dispute with his family, he travels west to see the place for himself, and from that experience he ostensibly spins another tale. This one deals with the adventures of Billy Bone, a rich character that maintains the folkloric appeal as a dime-novel figure. The novel derives its irony from its point of view. Its narrator is an architect of exaggeration and falsehood, but he presents this story as a personal narrative full of self-criticism. Sippy paints himself as psychologically unbalanced, immature, inadequate to life in the West, and at the same time imaginative and sympathetic. Given the date of its composition, around the time McMurtry was writing the *Lonesome Dove* saga, it is not surprising to encounter the same stark ambivalence toward the mythology of the American West in both works. In *Anything for Billy,* that tension is more obvious, taking the form of satire.

The novel (not atypical of McMurtry's work) is essentially a plotless series of episodes involving a group of interesting characters, and the book's appeal lies primarily in their interaction and dialogue, in the manner in which they appeal to the reader while at the same time ironically challenging the patterns of the dime-novel genre. The short chapters contain what are essentially vignettes and ministories, often involving action and the characters' reaction to it and usually ending with a pithy and sometimes poignant line. Figures such as Ben Sippy, Billy Bone, Joe Lovelady, the rancher Will Insinglass, his henchman Mesty-Woolah, and Katie Garza invest the novel with a humor that is essentially tragic, as all the characters, in predictable McMurtry fashion, struggle against personal and natural circumstances they cannot control. Of course, two figures stand out, the dime novelist Ben Sippy and Billy Bone himself. Sippy is careful to outline and describe the various books he has written, but he makes it clear that *Anything for Billy* is a memoir (fictional, of course) rather than a dime novel. He thus adopts realism as a mode and promises to treat his material honestly. He is most honest about himself: "The extraordinary thing about Will Isinglass was that, to an uncommon degree, he forced life to honor his expectations. Most of us can't do that—I'm a prime example of one who can't. My own expectations are apt to soar and dip, depending on the direction and stiffness of the breeze" (75). In Will Insinglass, a fictional blend of a host of ranchers and industrialists (most notably John Chisum), McMurtry acknowledges the possibility of agency and force of will, even in a largely deterministic world. But Sippy characterizes himself in antiheroic terms, while at the same time ruefully pointing out that he has written the most popular dime novel in the world. With a certain degree of comfort, Sippy accepts his lack of authority over his future and takes a confident pleasure in the fact that he is similar to most people, even (as the novel plays out) his most colorful yet problematic heroes, Billy and Joe. This antiheroic posture is presented to the reader as the narrator's honest characterization of himself and contributes to the pervasive irony and sadness of the novel. In essence, McMurtry performs a loving critique of the very process and source of popular mythology, of the Western in particular. This appears particularly as he characterizes Billy Bone:

> Billy expected people to take note of his reputation, though why he even had a reputation at the time was a mystery to me, once I knew the facts. From listening to gossip in barrooms I had formed the general impression that he had already killed ten or twelve white men, and scores of Indians and Mexicans as well.
>
> But when I met him, Billy Bone had yet to shoot a man. A bully named Joe Loxton had abused him considerably when he was thirteen or fourteen and making his living cleaning tables in a saloon. Joe Loxton made the mistake of wrestling him to the ground one day when Billy had just been carving beef and happened to have a butcher knife in his hand. When they hit the floor the butcher knife stuck in Joe Loxton's belly, and a day or two later he was dead.
>
> "It was mostly an accident," Billy said, "though I *would* have stabbed that shit-ass if I'd had time to think."
>
> That is not to say that Billy was a gentle boy. He was violent all right. In his case the reputation just arrived before the violence. (6–7)

"Once I knew the facts" playfully signals readers, warning them to be aware of the dissonance between reality and myth, truth and gossip. It is interesting here that mythogenesis itself is associated with a gossip chain, rather than with the developed oral traditions from which we often consider it to have emerged. In the incident with Joe Loxton, McMurtry provides a vivid picture of how facts can be distorted in service of myth and reputation, and what is more fascinating is how the case of Billy Bone posits a subtle theory as to one potential source of violence itself. Billy cares about his reputation before he genuinely embodies it, and it is likely the case that the reputation becomes the strongest motivator to violent acts, especially when the circumstances of the Whisky Glass War present the opportunity. Thus the process of myth creation is revealed in a richly human and realist context. But, even in that self-reflexive criticism, there is sympathy for his subject and a respect for the genuine experience that has given rise to the myth.

The central character, Billy Bone, who is clearly Billy the Kid, is so large in the historical imagination that the historical figure himself exists inseparable from the myth. He was a brash young man, devoid of upbringing and family, who found himself caught in a range war and had an instinct for violence and brutality. McMurtry is aware that the historical Billy and the mythic Billy co-exist in the Western imagination, and in the novel he seeks to lend him color and a degree of sympathy and humanity without shrinking from the reality of his sordid life. In describing the gunfighters in the town of Greasy Corners, McMurtry elucidates Billy's character:

> The rest were frankly just the journeyman of the owlhoot trail—a jolly lot when jolly and a sullen lot when sullen.
>
> All of them—even Hill Coe—were careful of Billy Bone, a boy with little experience, but with a reckless eye.
>
> They don't know what Billy might do," was Joe Lovelady's analysis. "They don't and he don't neither." (79)

Billy emerges not as a man of skill and calm, the cool killer of Western myth, but as an impetuous youth given to acts of kindness, humor, as well as to unpredictability and violence. In the countermyth created through the use of Ben Sippy as narrator, Billy is essentially a boy, one of brutish impulse, perhaps, but also a product of circumstance, as the West becomes a place for the unwanted, for outcasts, orphans, and misfits. Early on, Ben Sippy writes that there was a time when he would have done "anything for Billy," and in rendering his story Sippy displays a considerable skill in creating a character with complexity and nuance. It is in this sense that Sippy is perhaps a consciously constructed a stand-in for McMurtry himself, a teller of tales who exists in odd relation to his material: the bookish, thoughtful, and romantic artist who is capable of comprehending and truthfully treating the reality of lives that exist beneath a veneer of myth.

Buffalo Girls (1990)

In another novel set in the American West and based on the life of a figure that has become central to American popular mythology, *Buffalo Girls*, with its roots in the dime novel, continues McMurtry's critical scrutiny of the Western. The novel's name is taken from a popular folksong, "Buffalo Gals," and it acknowledges the imaginative and folkloric appeal of the characters Calamity Jane (Martha Jane Canary), Dora DuFran, and Annie Oakley, along with their male compatriots, including Wild Bill Hickok. But *Buffalo Girls,* even more than *Anything for Billy,* becomes a tragic and scathing critique of the myth as well as of the human beings that gave rise to it. The novel is written in epistolary form, as Calamity Jane pens an extended account of her life addressed to the daughter she has given away. Jane claims to be writing the truth, and the personal nature of the letter form lends a sense of honesty and legitimacy to this assertion. In spite of her rather unenviable circumstances, she recognizes that she will form the substance of a dubious history. Implicit in this claim is that in writing these letters she will provide the "true" story of her life and circumstances, but a careful inquiry into the life of the historical Calamity Jane indicates that she was decent and generous but also given to tall tales about her circumstances. Her primary role in Buffalo Bill's Wild West Show was to embellish her life in story for the entertainment of an audience. Arguably, even from McMurtry's point of view (which is likely the reason he chose the epistolary form), her story is a mix of truth and exaggeration, perhaps motivated by a desire to gain her daughter's sympathy. In this context, the novel works as a critical comment on the act of historical representation. In her letter, Jane herself warns against the histories that will be written about her, but her own account is equally questionable. In this sense, McMurtry certainly levels a serious critique of the process by which figures are transformed into myths, but he also questions the objectivity of any history, given the fact that human investment in the past—at a sentimental, psychological, or ideological level—is likely to be imbued with the values, interests, and subjective perspectives of the historians themselves. Thus, there is a certain thematic weight to *Buffalo Girls* that in many ways is not obvious on an initial reading.

The novel begins toward the end of Calamity Jane's storied career as a scout and an Indian fighter. She is living temporarily in Deadwood, South Dakota, where she meets with a number of old compatriots, including Wild Bill Hickok. She becomes pregnant with his child (there is no evidence that he was actually the father of her child). He is shot in a bar and dies, and after the child his born she decides to give the child up for adoption to a couple from England. She becomes the confidante of Dora DuFran, the local madam. Dora is in love with a local cowboy but refuses to marry him because of a tragedy in her past, and he goes on to marry someone else in spite of his affection for Dora. After a time, Calamity Jane agrees to join Buffalo Bill's Wild West Show as it travels to England, where she hopes to see her daughter. The balance of the novel charts her conflicts in this regard and her inevitable decline.

The primary thrust of the narrative is to reveal the underlying truths of the dime-novel genre and the dissonance between story and reality. The female characters are certainly to be admired. They are independent and, in their own ways, strong. But their circumstances are degraded. Jane is an alcoholic and a wanderer, unable even to take care of her own child. Dora is a madam with a sad history. Annie Oakley is less desperate but is revealed as primarily a performer rather than a genuine woman of the frontier, given that she is seen only in the context of Buffalo Bill's campy and exaggerated show. In this sense, the novel works to dismantle the Western story, revealing it as other McMurtry novels have, only in this case more directly and with less ambivalence. Coming later than *Lonesome Dove*, *Buffalo Girls* invites readers to ponder their own perception of the West, a region that that they know primarily through the cheapest and most shallow renderings of the frontier myth. Characters emerge as tragically sympathetic and deeply vulnerable, victims of their own weaknesses and subject to situations that circumscribe their fates, even to their detriment. The West emerges as a place of wildness and freedom but equally as a place of degradation and despair. The novel reveals Calamity Jane in midlife, and we know she will wander aimlessly to her dying day, drinking and fabricating tales of her exploits to increasingly shrinking groups of listeners. She will die at fifty-one years of age of alcoholism and pneumonia, having abandoned at least one child in a vague search for place and meaning. Indeed, it is one of the most common stories that emerges from the West, as it relates not only to frontier heroes but also to conventional settlers and fortune seekers, those who collectively define in human terms the complex and compelling reality of American expansion in the nineteenth century.

Novels

McMurtry's output in the realm of the novel is nothing short of extraordinary, especially when one considers his work in other genres such as essays and screenplays. He has written a number of independent novels with new characters as well as books that deal with character more fully considered in his major works. In *Some Can Whistle* (1989), McMurtry reintroduced his most autobiographical character, Danny Deck of *All My Friends Are Going to Be Strangers*. In the earlier novel, the character achieves success as a novelist and sits on the cusp of a career much like McMurtry's own, but in spite of this success Danny feels dislocated from community and particularly love. At the end of the latter novel, Danny drowns the manuscript of his second novel in the Rio Grande River. Among McMurtry readers, there was some speculation that Danny Deck had died, speculation prompted by the tragic musings of his fictional sometime lover, Emma Horton. But in *Some Can Whistle* he reappears alive, years later, at age fifty-one, as a successful but disillusioned multimillionaire who has made his fortune as a scriptwriter for the highly successful sitcom *Al and Sal,* which deals in comic terms with a recognizably ordinary family. It is part of the comic irony of the novel that he has achieved monumental success writing about something he has not experienced, since he has remained single and in part intentionally cultivated a separation from family and community. He has had a number of relationships with actresses, but he remains isolated, communicating primarily by answering machines. The novel places in tension the themes of family and community on one hand and isolation and individualism on the other, weighing in in favor of the former. In this sense, *Some Can Whistle* tends to scrutinize the legitimacy of the American ideal of individualism, which is in many ways derived from the frontier mythology McMurtry has critically explored all along.

Evening Star (1992) is an independent addition to the novels of the Houston Trilogy. *Moving On, All My Friends Are Going to Be Strangers,* and *Terms of Endearment* are in a sense a single unit, bound in theme, content, and the time frame of setting and publication. *Evening Star* continues the story of Aurora Greenway, many years after the events of *Terms of Endearment,* as she struggles mentally with the reality of old age and continues many of her endearing but dissipated behaviors. He main suitor in *Terms of Endearment* is General Hector Scott, and, as in the previous novel, in *Evening Star* they live together in a tentative arrangement, along with Aurora's maid Rosie. But, though quite old now, Aurora continues to be preoccupied with youth, behaving as if she were much younger as she continues to attract and manipulate suitors, including, most interestingly, a lay psychoanalyst decades younger than she. The novel continues McMurtry's practice of eschewing tight plots in favor of incident and the realistic portrayal of often directionless life situations. The novel's primary theme is the inevitability of aging and death, and Aurora achieves a kind of pathos in her struggle to maintain herself in the face of inevitability.

Other McMurtry novels include *Somebody's Darling* (1978), *Cadillac Jack* (1982), and *The Desert Rose* (1983), as well as *The Late Child* (1995), which is a sequel to *The Desert Rose.* All of these works, and a number of others he has written, are, perhaps with some justification, less highly regarded by critics than the books that are considered McMurtry's major efforts, but they do advance in many ways his major themes. *Somebody's Darling* involves characters from the Houston Trilogy, and all of them deal with the confrontation with modernity in various forms and the inevitable human malaise that emerges from this interaction, as characters move directionless through the dissipated locales of Hollywood, Las Vegas, and Houston. In *The Late Child,* Harmony is an aging Las Vegas showgirl who must face the fact that her daughter, Pepper, will not replace her on stage. Later, Harmony learns that Pepper has died of AIDS in New York, and she must endure the grief and loneliness, though with help from her sisters she finds new meaning in her young son, Eddie, the "late child" from whom the novel's title is derived. These and other works, written at various times throughout McMurtry's career, contribute to his corpus in various ways, particularly as the lesser novels provide an optic though which to read the more substantial works that constitute his various sagas.

Among these sagas is an extended series of novels referred to as the Berrybender Narratives, which include *Sin Killer* (2002), *The Wandering Hill* (2003), *By Sorrow's River* (2003), and *Folly and Glory* (2004). All of these novels are American historical romances and frontier narratives, offering McMurtry's unique and often sardonic treatment of characters traveling and coping in various places throughout the American West. The narratives are set in the mid-1830s and center on the members of an aristocratic English hunting party, the Berrybenders, as they travel across the West. Each novel traces the group's journey to and along a different river, and by the fourth novel the Berrybenders, injured and having suffered many losses, find their way wounded to the Rio Grande River while attempting to find Santa Fe. They have suffered significantly in the long and strangely antiheroic journey. Their leader, Lord Berrybender, has lost limbs and experienced other injuries. His wife and a number of his children have died, along with many servants, tutors, and hired hunters. The first novel, *Sin Killer,* is set in 1832 as the party begins its expedition. The title refers to the nickname of the character Jim Snow, who travels with them and violently hates "sin" in all its forms. *The Wandering Hill* is set in 1833 and recounts the Berrybenders' journey to the Yellowstone River and into the Rocky Mountains. The title refers to an ominous movable hill from Native American legend. The hill is rumored to appear at scenes of tragedy and suggests the ill-conceived nature of the journey the Berrybenders have undertaken. *By Sorrow's River* is also set in 1833 and recounts the group's journey south through the Great Plains, through Bent's Fort, and finally to the Arkansas River. The novel heightens the chance nature of tragedy and death and significantly emphasizes the antiheroic and absurd nature of the trip the Berrybenders have undertaken and their limitations as they attempt to control their circumstances. *Folly and Glory* concludes the Berrybenders' "adventure" as they move from Santa Fe to war-torn Texas and New Mexico, as many in the group face tragedy and destruction both internally and externally.

In the Berrybender Narratives, McMurtry takes great care to render the West and the Western experience in antimythic terms. The exploits of the group include a series of tragic mishaps that reveal the constant thwarting of the characters' intentions. There is little if any human agency in the world of these novels, and the harshness of the land seems a central theme. The characters are endearing and pathetic and demonstrate little significant overt conventional heroism, which becomes apparent in their lack of agency. The tone of the novels is bleak and sardonic, dominated by a less-than-subtle comic sensibility. McMurtry makes certain in these frontier "Westerns" to undermine the American mythology that began with James Fenimore Cooper and characterized the work of later frontier writers; he defines heroism in more starkly modern terms, through individual heroes' stoic response to the circumstances that dictate their fate.

Nonfiction

One unique thing about Larry McMurtry has been his willingness to reflect upon his writing process and on the subject matter that compels him. Again, he is clearly drawn to region, and his exploration of place appears in a number of essay collections, particularly *In a Narrow Grave: Essays on Texas* (1968), *Flim Flam: Essays on Hollywood* (1987), *Walter Benjamin at the Dairy Queen: Reflections on Sixty and Beyond* (1999), and *Sacagawea's Nickname: Essays on the American West* (2001). Specifically germane to the themes of his novels is his first collection, *In a Narrow Grave*. The book begins with a preface written for the first publication in 1968, but a 1989 edition contains an updated preface, in which McMurtry clarifies his motives for writing the collection and provides some details regarding its history. He frankly admits that the collection was a bit of an afterthought and that, besides the foreword and introduction, only three essays were written specifically for the volume. But, after writing his first three novels, he clearly felt the need to deal with the subject of Texas outside the context of fiction, to lift the veil so to speak, and address his readers directly, in a calmly poetic yet conversational style. In the first essay, "An Introduction: The God Abandons Texas," he candidly addresses a part of his purpose: "I started, indeed, to call the book *The Cowboy and the Suburb*, but chose the present title instead because I wanted a tone that was elegiac rather than sociological" (xxi). With regard to his themes and aesthetic practice as a whole, this comment is telling, if not revelatory. In the context of the social novel, the tension between the elegiac and the sociological is ever-present, and the negotiation between the two is the writer's perpetual task. McMurtry is aware of the sociological and historical content of his works and by no means works against it, sometimes weighing in in favor of the elegiac only in his careful choice of title. But throughout the collection, he maintains an emphasis on the artist's power to illuminate the social sphere, and he does so notably as he contemplates the history and social texture of his region. In the same introduction, referring to nineteenth- and twentieth-century Texas and the evolution from rural to urban cultures, he wrote, "The death, however, moves me—the way of life that is dying had its value. Its appeal was simple, but genuine, and it called to it and is taking with it people whom one could not but love" (xxi).

This statement expresses many of the central themes of the early novels, themes that continue and become more complex in the later work. The elegiac sensibility is present in the statement, and in the essays he maintained this tone while anticipating the self-reflexive irony so evident in the Houston Trilogy and the *Lonesome Dove* saga. In one of the opening essays, "Here's Hud in Your Eye," he reflects on the film adaptation of his first novel, *Horseman, Pass By*. He has a guarded respect for the adaptation and in challenging it takes responsibility for what he sees as the excessive sentimentality of its source material. He does see the main character, Hud, as a dark modern manifestation of the gunfighter and cowboy, but the essay seems less a lament on the figure's passing and more a strident critique of what he has become, since the modern world has muted the justification for violence. In the preface to the 1989 edition, McMurtry acknowledges that three of the other essays genuinely stand out, since from the inception he intended to include them in the volume. These are "Southwestern Literature?," "Eros in Archer County," and "Take My Saddle from the Wall: A Valediction." In many ways, given the subsequent development of Western literature as an academic subfield and the massive growth of a Western literary canon, the essay on Southwestern writers is a bit dated. However, the piece functions as a call for the development and consideration of this regional tradition; one of McMurtry's major assertions is that the region, and Texas specifically, is worthy of literary attention. McMurtry acknowledges that rural Texas is not particularly bookish or intellectual, but he laments the fact that authors who come from Texas have frequently been drawn to other, perhaps more urban spaces. He focuses specifically on the work of Roy Bedichek, W. P. Webb, and J. Frank Dobie, writers who tend not to dominate the current canon of Western American literature. But McMurtry's ruminations on the value of place and the manner in which these authors call attention to it function in many ways as a foundational statement on the need for writers to focus on region and for scholars to consider their work. Though his professed claim for the volume is that it weigh in the direction of the elegiac rather than the sociological, "Eros in Archer County" is a sociological study thinly veiled as a personal narrative. McMurtry comments on everything from the evolution of sexual attitudes in Texas from the nineteenth into the twentieth centuries and gender codes with respect to sexuality to what it was like to grow up within the context of a culture in which sex was a taboo subject of conversation and was frankly little understood, even by adults. Again, he treats Texas as an overt metonym for modern American culture as a whole, particularly in rural areas, as the country undergoes a wrenching social and collectively psychological transformation in values, codes, and mores. "Take My Saddle from the Wall: A Valediction" is ostensibly a reflection on three generations of his family, with special attention paid to his father's generation. But it emerges as a balanced inquiry into the myth of the cowboy and the power and limitations the myth imposes on those who choose to live by it. He includes a letter from his maternal uncle, whose wife has died in a car accident. The uncle is clearly affected by the loss but in the letter puts as much emphasis on the loss of his car. McMurtry identifies this stoicism with the cowboy myth, one that is essentially "Roman," and he associates it explicitly with Seneca. McMurtry emphasizes cowboys' idealization of women—their desire for women and their discomfort in communicating with them. In all, he displays a measured respect for the myth while recognizing, in this case quite elegiacally, its inevitable decline and transformation.

In a Narrow Grave deals with the change from an older social order into a new one, and *Walter Benjamin at the Dairy Queen: Reflections on Sixty and Beyond* (1999) grounds those issues at a personal level. His work on the collection began after his bypass surgery and reflects the obvious concerns of a writer now fully aware of his vulnerability and mortality. McMurtry's own life is the locus of change. He was apparently inspired by a moment when he was drinking a lime Dr Pepper at a Dairy Queen on Highway 79 north of Archer City and connected his experience there to a book by Walter Benjamin, the European literary critic, who wrote among other things about the value of the storyteller. The collection deals with four major themes or phases that apply to McMurtry's own life, which he organizes into chapters. The first, "Place—and Memories of Place," begins with his reading of Benjamin and moves to a contemplation of place as McMurtry has come to experience it in Archer City, particularly as it relates to his family's connection to the locale. Place and its role in recollection become a central feature of identity. He notices that the Dairy Queen itself is a locus of storytelling in the community and he reflects on the differences between this natural phenomenon in community and his role as a single teller of written stories in the form of the novel. The second chapter, "Reading," deals with those times in McMurtry's life when he wasn't involved in the act of storytelling himself; he reflects on the strange fact that he became an avid reader even though the environment in which he grew up was rather anti-intellectual. He recounts anecdotes and details of how his reading life emerged—from a collection of books left to him by his cousin, to books found on drugstore racks, to his reading in college. The third chapter, "Book Scouting," extends the emphasis on reading as McMurtry charts his experiences as a book scout and book collector, which ultimately led to his opening bookstores. Chapter 4, "The End of the Cowboy—the End of Fiction," is particularly pertinent in terms of McMurtry's Western themes. In this section, McMurtry draws parallels between his own life as a writer and his father's life as a rancher. His father's enterprise was ultimately doomed, since it depended on an imported animal rather than the native bison. McMurtry compares that activity to his own (he assumes) failure to fully demythologize the West. The collection takes the idea of memory and reflection as primary theme and, in the process, reveals much of what has motivated McMurtry as an author.

McMurtry has also written memoirs that deal not only with the textured reality of place but with his own reaction to it as a writer and reader. These memoirs include *Roads: Driving America's Highways* (2000) and *Paradise* (2001). Both center on the act of journeying but in many ways lack an emphasis on the genuine travel element. *Roads* deals with a series of drives along America's highways that involve brief and in many ways inconsequential encounters with various well-known landmarks. But McMurtry's sensibility finds more compelling other, less-considered locations, many having to do with the writers and readers: James Agee's Knoxville, William Faulkner's Mississippi, Ernest Hemingway's Key West, Michigan, and Idaho. It becomes less a conventional travel book and more a narrative of interior preoccupation, as McMurtry records his impression of the places that have been important to him as a writer. He gives particular attention to the places where he has lived and worked—Washington, D.C., and Archer County, Texas. *Paradise* is another ostensible "travel" narrative that involves an interior rather than an exterior journey. It begins on board the freighter *Aranui,* which sails out of Tahiti. On the surface this is a book about visiting the South Sea islands of Gauguin and Melville, but the nonfiction narrative involves a figurative dimension taken from the writer's own experience. His observations of the destructive nature of capitalist enterprise are easily applied to his own experiences in Texas and to the themes he has explored in his many novels. In that context, he observes those who travel with him with a clear ambivalence, an ambivalence that registers his observation of the difference between the South Sea islands of the artists, writers, and explorers he admires and their reality in the modern world. It is certainly a travel book, but one that is imbued and ultimately concerned with his own lifetime of experience and memory, as his own distinctive choices and observations color his writing about the islands. His experience and perspective are unique, given that he was brought up on a ranch and in a small Texas town and was raised amid the tensions of ranching culture, oil culture, and the

American small town. These same tensions find their way into his observations of people and place in *Paradise,* as the writer yet again encounters a world that simultaneously attracts and repels him.

In the realm of nonfiction, Larry McMurtry is a writer of notable accomplishment, and though his reputation as a novelist is considerable, his output as an essayist places him among a select few writers known particularly for their nonfiction. His collection of essays *Sacagawea's Nickname: Essays on the American West* continues the focus on region that began with *In a Narrow Grave.* Throughout his career, McMurtry has reviewed books for numerous journals and magazines, and in later years he began writing review essays for the *New York Review of Books. Sacagawea's Nickname* brings those essays together in a single volume, and though they are certainly reviews, McMurtry also contemplates issues and concerns that the books he is presumably reviewing bring to mind. The twelve essays in the volume deal with books written about the American West and focusing on topics such as historical figures, including John Wesley Powell, the explorer of the Colorado River; entertainers and figures of Western myth such as Buffalo Bill and Annie Oakley; and the writer Zane Grey. The essays deal also with the tragic dispossession of Native Americans, particularly the Five Civilized Tribes and the Zuni Pueblo, and the work of anthropologists and historians such as Angie Debo and Patricia Nelson Limerick. There are also two essays dealing with the Lewis and Clark Expedition. The essay from which the volume takes its title is derived from *The Journals of Lewis and Clark* and involves a speculative exploration into the relationship between William Clark and Sacagawea, whom he first called "squaw" and later "Janey." The contours of their interaction are only thinly rendered in the journal, and McMurtry employs his considerable talents as a creator of character to give dimension to Clark, Sacagawea, and their relationship. In many ways, it is through his nonfiction that the reader gets a vivid image of McMurtry's personality and sensibility. He is clearly a man of incisive wit and strong opinion, full of sardonic humor and more than a little cynicism with regard to the nature of human beings and the realities of the modern condition. But he observes with vision and presents the world as he sees it with honesty and clarity of insight. The essays provide a context through which one can read his fiction, but they also stand on their own as nuanced inquiries into the modern condition and the particularities of place.

Collaboration: Larry McMurtry and Diana Ossana

McMurtry has collaborated on a number of screenplays and worked together with other creative people in adapting his novels for film, but his most significant collaboration has been with Diana Ossana. McMurtry met Ossana in the mid-1980s at a Mr. Catfish restaurant in Tucson, Arizona. He had spent time in Tucson in the 1970s and in the early 1990s opened another bookstore there and expanded it into an antique store. At the time they met, Ossana, an Italian American from St. Louis who attended Eastern New Mexico University, was working as the manager of a law office. Their collaboration led to two significant works, *Pretty Boy Floyd* (1994) and *Zeke and Ned* (1997). It is difficult to know what motivated the collaboration, but McMurtry and Ossana became longtime companions, and he often complained about the isolation of writing in the context of remembering the working relationships he observed among the cowboys around whom he grew up. But it is clear that the personal and working relationship between the two authors was valuable to both, and it was Ossana who helped McMurtry through his recovery from bypass surgery and the depression that followed. McMurtry describes the particular process of collaboration in this way: "I write five pages early. Diana makes them ten, a little later. My narrative is spare, she expands it. It is full of collaboration, meaning the division of labor is as equal as equal can be. We work on it together, and we work on it separately, as well. We researched it together."

In a Collaborator's Note that introduces *Pretty Boy Floyd,* the authors wrote that the novel began as a screenplay for Warner Brothers in 1993 but that the form of the screenplay did not allow for the detail permitted by the novel. *Pretty Boy Floyd* is a narrative that charts the experiences and develops the complex character of Charles Arthur Floyd, the well-known Depression-era outlaw, as he evolved from a humble farm boy from Salisaw, Oklahoma, to become Public Enemy Number One on J. Edgar Hoover's list of most-wanted criminals in 1934. In the novel, Floyd is presented in deeply human terms. Initially, he is a decent family man caught in the grip of the Great Depression. The novel is organized around a series of journeys and deals with the events that led the young man to become an outlaw, introducing a number of other characters. Floyd is presented to some degree as a victim of history, as the times themselves in part prompted him to become a bank robber. The novel thus is a critique of the rampant materialism that led to economic catastrophe and to the media culture that elevated outlaws to mythic status, though McMurtry and Ossana in some ways affirm the myth. The narrative is noticeably different from works McMurtry wrote alone, given its particular emphasis on the era and the departure from his common themes of transition from the nineteenth to the twentieth centuries.

McMurtry and Ossana's collaboration continued with the publication, three years later, of *Zeke and Ned*. Though McMurtry's practice has been to deliberately demythologize the West, in these two books coauthored with Ossana there is a degree of (often playful) mythogenesis. Zeke and Ned, two

Cherokees, become in many ways positive mythic types. Ned Christie is full of mythic traits: strength, wisdom, honesty, and skill with a gun. He defends his family against a group of hapless white men with dubious motives. Zeke is older and more humanly drawn but still remains a heroic figure, particularly in comparison with the antagonists. In fact, Ned Christie and Zeke Proctor were historical figures who lived in the Indian Territory in the late 1800s, and the general outlines of their experiences are rendered accurately. In the novel in particular, the two men live rather conventional lives in the Going Snake District of the Cherokee Indian Nation Territory. Zeke is taken to trial in a Cherokee court for an accidental killing, resulting in the shootout that leads to the decimation of Zeke's family and initiates Ned Christie into the life that makes him the most famous outlaw of the Cherokee Nation. McMurtry and Ossana's tendency to render their heroes in mythological terms, as they did also with Pretty Boy Floyd, is in many ways explained by the tragic circumstances each character confronts, and in this sense McMurtry's common theme regarding the power of history to circumscribe lives finds its way into his collaboration with Ossana. It was a collaboration that was valuable for both authors, and for McMurtry it seemed to mitigate the sense of isolation he often felt as a writer. Their collaboration continued in 1996, when Ossana was the cowriter of the screenplay for *Dead Man's Walk*.

Epilogue

In the second decade of the twenty-first century, after writing for more than fifty years, Larry McMurtry remains one of America's most prolific contemporary authors. McMurtry's themes are by no means narrow, but, even considering the significant number of novels and essay collections, he remains true to his concern with Texas as a metonym for the American experience as a whole. Issues of modernity, transience, sweeping and often cataclysmic social change, and the inevitable, dramatic, but always consequential effects of these changes are central to his concerns. In his complex characterizations, these effects are quite subtle, and the characters themselves are often only vaguely aware of the source of their concerns and dilemmas. They do their best to cope and adapt and can do so with only a certain limited success; they survive and find meaning often only tentatively, frequently in the context of work that is motivated by deeply rooted values that are sometimes lacking in contemporary relevance. In this context the characters achieve a kind of sympathy and beauty. Sometimes even within individual novels such as *Moving On*, McMurtry alternates between the urban and the rural, exploring the complementary dreams of people who live in both locales, charting with sympathy the natural tensions that exist as two contradictory modes of living, together with different material values, come into regular contact and must at times integrate and blend. There is a quality of bittersweet tragedy that pervades all of his works, as characters struggle and frequently fail to adapt to the inherent transience that is characteristic of America in the twentieth and twenty-first centuries, a transience typical as well of all times and all histories, of the human experience writ large.

In many ways, Larry McMurtry stands out among contemporary writers, and contemporary literary scholars have sometimes been ambivalent about his work. His background and education make it clear that he is more familiar than many of his contemporaries with the Euro-American literary tradition from the ancient period through the twentieth century. But he has intentionally eschewed the narrative experimentation and complex narrative strategies that are a central part of the modernist legacy. He seems less concerned with philosophical and metaphysical questions than are many writers of the late twentieth century, and his prose is simple, direct, and eminently clear. He is in every way a stylist, and any reader of a McMurtry paragraph will quickly observe the distinctiveness of that style. But his language does not call attention to itself. For all of these reasons he has attained a popularity that surpasses that of most writers today who are considered important, and in some ways this has worked against his reputation among academics.

In the end, however, his value is significant and undisputable, especially when one is considering the history of literary canonization and his predecessors. Avoiding the narrative conventions and thematic preoccupations of philosophical and metaphysical romancers of unmistakable value such as Herman Melville, William Faulkner, and Cormac McCarthy, he has chosen to explore human beings in a rich but comprehensible historical and cultural context. He shares this approach with authors such as Jane Austen, Charles Dickens, George Eliot, and many others who worked in the tradition of the social novel and who were tremendously popular yet later emerged as significant subjects of academic study.

It remains to consider what distinguishes McMurtry's work from that of other popular authors of his time. Most notable is his emphasis on character and characters' relationships. When not driven by a journey narrative or the simple organizing principle of time, McMurtry's novels are often plotless. Certainly sequence and causality figure in his narratives, but rarely do we find the heightening of conflict typical of a conventional plot. The internal and external conflicts of characters are frequently as unpredictable and directionless as those we encounter in life; McMurtry is again primarily a novelist of social and psychological realism. In this sense, Larry McMurtry has taken significant aesthetic risks, writing novels that eschew plot, the most widely used mechanism in popular stories, without relying on the justification that naturally emerges from narrative experimentation and an association with modernism and its aftermath. That said, there is a thematic modernism clearly present in his work—the emphasis on radical social change, transience, psychological instability—and all have evoked the common comparison of McMurtry to William Faulkner. But these themes are not the exclusive property of modernism and have been central to the tradition of the novel and the Euro-American literary tradition broadly construed. In the exploration of these themes in the context of nineteenth- and twentieth-century America, Larry McMurtry is distinctive and by many accounts unexcelled. In an environment that often blurs the distinction between the people and the natural conditions that constrain them, he remains committed to revealing the rich, deep, and exquisitely textured reality of the human experience. Certainly one of the most dedicated authors of the late twentieth and early twenty-first centuries, Larry McMurtry holds a distinctive place among his fellows. On one hand, the surface level simplicity of many of his works conceals a deeper complexity. In his social novels, he is firmly a realist, but a realist in some ways like Henry James. McMurtry is a novelist preoccupied with the interiors of human consciousness and personality, an observer of the intricacies and foibles of individual identities. He is attentive to the nuances, the kind of distinctive-fingerprint nature of individual human beings in their reactions to themselves and to their world. In terms of the tradition of the novel of manners, he helps to initiate a genuine advance of the genre in ways that are often underrecognized. His episodic and sometimes directionless plots are in fact purposefully so, as they mirror the nature of contemporary experience in the wake of modernity, and he makes no attempt to clean them up for the reader through artificial and contrived conclusions. He thus writes for his reader's pleasure but never backs down from his mission to represent the truth as he sees it. In terms of his use of the American historical romance, he writes with an awareness of the tradition of frontier literature from the novels of James Fenimore Cooper through its transformation into the Western in film. At the center of this is mythogenesis and the reconsideration of the value of these myths. His scrutiny of the Western ideal is subtle and sometimes misunderstood, but a careful reading reveals a clearly antimythological sensibility motivated by an urgent desire to engage and challenges the extremes of the American imperial project. As a popular writer, Larry McMurtry has achieved tremendous success, and in a number of major works he has made a significant and increasingly obvious contribution to the American literary tradition.

NOTES

Chapter 1—Understanding Larry McMurtry

1. See Mark Busby, *Larry McMurtry and the West: An Ambivalent Relationship* (Denton: University of North Texas Press, 1995).

2. Mervyn Rothstein, "A Texan Who Likes to Deflate the Legends of the Golden West." *New York Times Book Review.* 1 Nov. 2015. http://www.nytimes/1988/11/01/books/a-texan-who-likes-to-deflate-the-legends-of-the-golden-west.html

3. For a detailed consideration of the dime novel in the context of the mythology of the American west, see Henry Nash Smith's *Virginland: The American West as Symbol and Myth* (Cambridge, Mass.: Harvard University Press, 1970).

4. See Richard Slotkin, *Gunfighter Nation: The Myth of the Frontier in Twentieth-Century America* (New York: Atheneum, 1992).

5. See Roger Jones, *Larry McMurtry and the Victorian Novel* (College Station: Texas A&M University Press), 1994.

6. For a discussion of the controversy surrounding Chase's thesis and a detailed affirmation of Chase's distinction between the novel and the romance derived from the archives, see G. R. Thompson and Eric Carl Link's *Neutral Ground: New Traditionalism and the American Romance Controversy* (Baton Rouge: Louisiana State University Press, 1999).

Chapter 2—The Early Works

1. See Mark Busby, "Damn the Saddle on the Wall: Anti-Myth in Larry McMurtry's *Horseman, Pass By*." *New Mexico Humanities Review* 3 (1980): 5–10.

2. Marshall Sprague, "Texas Triptych." *New York Times Book Review.* 4 Nov. 2015. http://www.nytimes.com/books/97/12/07/home/mcmurtry-cheyenne.html

Chapter 3—The Thalia Novels

1. Thomas Lask, "Books of the Times." *New York Times Book Review.* 5 Nov. 2015. http://www.nytimes.com/book/97/12/07/home/mcmurtry-show.html

2. David Evans, "Lights, Camera, and Gentle, Comic Action." *Independent.* 5 Nov. 2015. http://www.independent.co.uk./arts-entertainment/books/reviews/the-last-picture-show.html

3. See Greg Giddings, "The Love Song of Larry McMurtry: *The Last Picture Show.*" *Journal of the American Studies Association of Texas* 44 (2013): 57–64.

4. See Daniel Woodward, "Larry McMurtry's *Texasville*: A Comic Pastoral of the Oil-Patch." *Huntington Library Quarterly* 56 (1993): 167–80.

5. Michiko Kakutani, "Books of the Times." *New York Times Book Review.* 8 April 1987. 24.

6. Jonathan Yardley, "Deep in the Heart of Larry McMurtry." *Washington Post Book World,* 12 April 1987. 3.

7. Louise Erdrich, "Why Is That Man Tired." *New York Times Book Review.* 8 Nov. 2015. http://www.nytimes.com/books/99/01/10/specials/mcmurtry-texasville.html

8. Nancy Pate, "Between the Lines." *Orlando Sentinel.* 24 Jan. 1999. 18.

9. Judith Wynn, "Duane's Depressed and We Are Better for It." *Boston Herald.* 24 Jan. 1999. 14.

Chapter 4—The Houston Trilogy

1. See Kerry Ahearn, "More D'Urban: The Texas Novels of Larry McMurtry." *Texas Quarterly* 19 (1976): 109–29.

2. John Leonard, "Books of the Times." *New York Times Book Review.* 8 Nov. 2015. http://www.nytimes.com/books/97/12/07/home/mcmurtry-moving.html

3. Jim Harrison, *"All My Friends Are Going to Be Strangers." New York Times Book Review.* 8 Nov. 2015. http://www.nytimes.com/books/97/12/07/home/mcmurtry-friends .html

4. Robert Towers, "An Oddly Misshapen Novel by a Highly Accomplished Novelist." *New York Times Book Review.* 8 Nov. 2015. http://www.nytimes.com/books/97/14/07/ home/mcmurtry-friends.html

5. Christopher Lehmann-Haupt, "Books of the Times." *New York Times Book Review.* 8 Nov. 2015. http://www.nytimes.com/books/97/12/07/home/mcmurtry-endearment .html

6. The novel is followed by a sequel, *Evening Star* (1999), that deals with Emma's children at older ages and their relationship with Aurora, but the thematic issues are different, and the book was written much later. As such, it is not often considered a part of the Houston Trilogy.

Chapter 5—The *Lonesome Dove* Saga

1. Mervyn Rothstein, "A Texan Who Likes to Deflate the Legend of the Golden West." *New York Times Book Review.* 11 Nov. 2015. http://www.nytimes/1988/11/01books/ a-texan-who-likes-to-deflate-the-legends-of-the-golden-west.html

2. See Deborah L. Madsen, "Discourses of Frontier Violence and the Trauma of National Emergence in Larry McMurtry's *Lonesome Dove* Quartet." *Review of American Studies* 39 (2009): 185–204.

3. John Horn, *Los Angeles Times Book Review.* 9 June 1985. 2.

4. See Christian Kiefer, "Unneighborly Behavior: *Blood Meridian, Lonesome Dove,* and the Problem of Reader Sympathy." *Southwestern American Literature* 33 (2007): 39–52.

5. For a discussion of the historical romance and its relation to the Waverley novels and the tension between the forces of progress and reaction, see George Dekker's *The American Historical Romance* (Cambridge: Cambridge University Press, 1987).

6. For a discussion of the early development of the American frontier hero, see Richard Slotkin's *Regeneration through Violence* (Norman: University of Oklahoma Press, 1973).

7. See J. Hector St. John de Crevecoeur's "Letter III" from *Letters from an American Farmer* and David Hackett Fisher's *Albion's Seed: Four British Folkways in America* (Oxford: Oxford University Press, 1989).

8. For a discussion of the history of the Comanche people, see S. C. Gwynne's *Empire of the Summer Moon: Quanah Parker and the Rise and Fall of the Comanches, the Most Powerful Indian Tribe in American History* (New York: Scribner's, 2011).

9. See Gwynne, *Empire of the Summer Moon.*

10. See Cordelia E. Barrera, "Written on the Body: A Third Space Reading of Larry McMurtry's *Streets of Laredo.*" *Western American Literature* 48 (2013): 232–52.

11. *Kirkus Reviews.* 1 June 1993.

12. Mark Horowitz, "How the West Was Done." *Los Angeles Times Book Review.* 8 Aug. 1993. 1.

13. Dee Brown, "The Return of Captain Call." *Chicago Sun-Times.* 12 Aug. 1993. 4.

14. Noel Perrin, "Woodrow Call Rides Again." *New York Times Book Review.* 11 Nov. 2015. http://www.nytimes.com/books/99/01/10/specials/mcmurtry-laraedo.html

15. Thomas Flanagan, "*Lonesome Dove:* The Prequel." *New York Times Book Review.* 11 Nov. 2015. http://www.nytimes.com/books/99/01/10/specials/mcmurtry-deadsman's.html

16. Andy Solomon, "Lonesome Dude." *New York Times Book Review.* 11 Nov. 2015. http://www.nytimes.com/books/97/12/07/reviews/971207.07solomot.html

SELECTED BIBLIOGRAPHY

Works by Larry McMurtry

INDIVIDUAL NOVELS

Horseman, Pass By. New York: Simon and Schuster, 1961.
Leaving Cheyenne. New York: Simon and Schuster, 1963.
Cadillac Jack. New York: Simon and Schuster, 1982.
Anything for Billy. New York: Simon and Schuster, 1988.
Buffalo Girls. New York: Simon and Schuster, 1990.
Pretty Boy Floyd. (co-author Diana Ossana). New York: Simon and Schuster, 1994.
Zeke and Ned. (co-author Diana Ossana). New York: Simon and Schuster, 1997.
Boone's Lick. New York: Simon and Schuster, 2000.
Loop Group. New York: Simon and Schuster, 2005.
Telegraph Days. New York: Simon and Schuster, 2006.
The Last Kind Words Saloon. New York: Liveright, 2014.

HARMONY & PEPPER SERIES

The Desert Rose. New York: Simon and Schuster, 1983.
The Late Child. New York: Simon and Schuster, 1995.

DUANE MOORE SERIES (THALIA SAGA)

The Last Picture Show. New York: Simon and Schuster, 1966.
Texasville. New York: Simon and Schuster, 1987.
Duane's Depressed. New York: Simon and Schuster, 1999.
When the Light Goes. New York: Simon and Schuster, 2007.
Rhino Ranch: A Novel. New York: Simon and Schuster, 2009.

HOUSTON NOVELS

Moving On. New York: Simon and Schuster, 1970.
All My Friends Are Going to Be Strangers. New York: Simon and Schuster, 1972.
Terms of Endearment. New York: Simon and Schuster, 1975.
Somebody's Darling. New York: Simon and Schuster, 1978.
Some Can Whistle. New York: Simon and Schuster, 1989.
The Evening Star. New York: Simon and Schuster, 1992.

THE *LONESOME DOVE* SAGA

Lonesome Dove. New York: Simon and Schuster, 1985; 1986 Pulitzer Prize.
Streets of Laredo. New York: Simon and Schuster, 1993.

Dead Man's Walk. New York: Simon and Schuster, 1995.
Comanche Moon. New York: Simon and Schuster, 1997.

BERRYBENDER NARRATIVES

Sin Killer. New York: Simon and Schuster, 2002.
The Wandering Hill. New York: Simon and Schuster, 2003.
By Sorrow's River. New York: Simon and Schuster, 2003.
Folly and Glory. New York: Simon and Schuster, 2004.

EDITED WORKS

Still Wild: A Collection of Western Stories. New York: Simon and Schuster, 1999.

FILMS AND SCREENPLAYS

The Murder of Mary Phagan (1988)—TV movie
Montana (1990)—TV movie
Memphis (1992)—TV movie
Falling from Grace (1992)—film starring John Mellencamp
Johnson County War (2002)—TV miniseries
Brokeback Mountain (with Diana Ossana; 2005)—Oscar-winning screenplay (adapted from the short story by E. Annie Proulx)

NONFICTION

In a Narrow Grave: Essays on Texas. New York: Simon and Schuster, 1968.
Film Flam: Essays on Hollywood. New York: Simon and Schuster, 1987.
Crazy Horse: A Life (biography). New York: Penguin, 1999.
Walter Benjamin at the Dairy Queen: Reflections on Sixty and Beyond. New York: Simon and Schuster, 1999.
Roads: Driving America's Great Highways. New York: Simon and Schuster, 2000.
Sacagawea's Nickname: Essays on the American West. New York: Simon and Schuster, 2001.
Paradise. New York: Simon and Schuster, 2002.
The Colonel and Little Missie: Buffalo Bill, Annie Oakley and the Beginnings of Superstardom in America. New York: Simon and Schuster, 2005.
Oh What a Slaughter! Massacres in the American West, 1846—1890. New York: Simon and Schuster, 2005.
Books: A Memoir. New York: Simon and Schuster, 2008.
Literary Life: A Second Memoir. New York: Simon and Schuster, 2009.
Hollywood: A Third Memoir. New York: Simon and Schuster, 2011.
Custer. New York: Simon and Schuster, 2012.

Works about Larry McMurtry

Ahearn, Kerry. "Larry McMurtry." In *Fifty Western Writers: A Bio-Bibliographic Sourcebook*. Ed. Fred Erisman and Richard Etulain. Westport, Conn.: Greenwood Press, 1992: 280–90.
Ahearn, Kerry. "More D'Urban: The Texas Novels of Larry McMurtry." *Texas Quarterly* 19 (Autumn 1976): 109–29; reprinted in *Critical Essays on the Western American Novel*, ed. William T. Pilkington. Boston: G. K. Hall, 1980: 223–42.

Barrera, Cordelia E. "Written on the Body: A Third Space Reading of Larry McMurtry's *Streets of Laredo*." *Western American Literature* 48 (Fall 2013): 232–52.

Busby, Mark. "Damn the Saddle on the Wall: Anti-Myth in Larry McMurtry's *Horseman, Pass By*." *New Mexico Humanities Review* 3 (Summer 1980): 5–10.

Busby, Mark. "Larry McMurtry." In *Twentieth-Century Western Writers*. Ed. James Vincent. Detroit: Gale, 1982: 534–36.

Busby, Mark. *Larry McMurtry and the West: An Ambivalent Relationship*. Denton: University of North Texas Press, 1995.

Clifford, Craig Edward. *In the Deep Heart's Core: Reflections on Life, Letters, and Texas*. College Station: Texas A&M Press, 2000.

Daigrepont, Lloyd M. "Passion, Romance, and Agape in Larry McMurtry's *Lonesome Dove*." *Lamar Journal of the Humanities* 30 (Fall 2005): 43–61.

Giddings, Greg. "*Lonesome Dove*: Butch and Sundance Go on a Cattledrive." *Southwestern American Literature* 12 (1986): 7–12.

Giddings, Greg. "The Love Song of Larry McMurtry: *The Last Picture Show*." *Journal of the American Studies Association of Texas* 44 (2013): 57–64.

Graham, Don. "Is Dallas Burning? Notes on Recent Texas Fiction." *Southwestern American Literature* 4 (1974): 68–73.

Hickey, Dave. "McMurtry's Elegant Essays." *Texas Observer* (7 February 1969): 14–16.

Huber, Dwight. "Larry McMurtry: A Selected Bibliography." In *Larry McMurtry: Unredeemed Dreams*. Ed. Dorey Smith, 15–37. Edinburg, Tex.: Pan American University Press, 1978.

Jones, Roger. *Larry McMurtry and the Victorian Novel*. College Station: Texas A&M University Press, 1994.

Kiefer, Christian. "Unneighborly Behavior: *Blood Meridian, Lonesome Dove*, and the Problem of Reader Sympathy." *Southwestern American Literature* 33 (Fall 2007): 39–52.

Landess, Thomas. *Larry McMurtry*. Austin: Steck-Vaughn, 1969.

Lich, Lera Patrick Tyler. *Larry McMurtry's Texas: Evolution of the Myth*. Austin: Eakin, 1987.

Madsen, Deborah L. "Discourses of Frontier Violence and the Trauma of National Emergence in Larry McMurtry's *Lonesome Dove* Quartet." *Review of American Studies* 39 (2009): 185–204.

Miller-Purrenhage, John. "'Kin to Nobody': The Disruption of Genealogy in Larry McMurtry's *Lonesome Dove*." *Critique: Studies in Contemporary Fiction* 47 (Fall 2005) 73–89.

Nelson, Jane. "Larry McMurtry." In *A Literary History of the American West*. Ed. J. Golden Taylor. Fort Worth: Texas Christian University Press, 1987: 612–21.

Peavy, Charles D. "A Larry McMurtry Bibliography. *Western American Literature* 8 (Fall 1968): 235–48.

Peavy, Charles. *Larry McMurtry*. Boston: Twayne/G. K. Hall, 1978.

Reid, Jan. "Return of the Native Son." *Texas Monthly* 21 (February 1993): 202, 228–31.

Reilly, John M. *Larry McMurtry: A Critical Companion*. Westport, Conn.: Greenwood, 2000.

Reynolds, Clay. *Taking Stock: A Larry McMurtry Casebook*. Dallas: Southern Methodist University Press, 1989.

Reynolds, R. C. "Back Trailing to Glory: *Lonesome Dove* and the Novels of Larry Mc-Murtry." *Texas Review* 8 (1987): 22–29.

Reynolds, R. C. "Come Home Larry, All Is Forgiven: A Native Son's Search for Identity." *Cross Timbers Review* 11 (May 1985): 65.

Sanderson, Jim. "Old Corals: Texas According to 80's Films and T.V. and Texas According to Larry McMurtry." *Journal of American Culture* 13 (Summer 1990): 63–73.

Schmidt, Dorey, ed. *Larry McMurtry: Unredeemed Dreams.* Edinburg, Tex.: Pan American University Press, 1978.

Sewell, Ernestine. "McMurtry's Cowboy-God in *Lonesome Dove.*" *Western American Literature* 21 (1986): 219–25.

Sonnichsen. C. L. *From Hopalong to Hud: Thoughts on Western Fiction.* College Station: Texas A&M University Press, 1978.

Stout, Janis P. "Cadillac Larry Rides Again: McMurtry and the Song of the Open Road." *Western American Literature* 24 (November 1989): 243–51.

Stout, Janis P. "Journeying as a Metaphor for Cultural Loss in the Novels of Larry Mc-Murtry." *Western American Literature* 11 (1976): 37–50.

Wilburn, David. "Dialogic Frontiers: History and Psychology in *Lonesome Dove* and *Blood Meridian.*" *Arizona Quarterly* 70 (Spring 2014): 81–108.

Williams, Charles. "Bibliography." *Taking Stock: A Larry McMurtry Casebook.* Ed. Clay Reynolds, 159–88. Dallas: Southern Methodist University Press, 1989.

Woodward, Daniel. "Larry McMurtry's *Texasville:* A Comic Pastoral of the Oil-Patch." *Huntington Library Quarterly* 56 (Spring 1993): 167–80.

INDEX